Spud Songs

Spud Songs

An Anthology
of Potato Poems

to Benefit Hunger Relief

Edited by
Gloria Vando & Robert Stewart

HELICON NINE EDITIONS
KANSAS CITY, MISSOURI

All rights reserved under International and Pan-American Copyright Conventions.
Published by the Midwest Center for the Literary Arts, Inc.
P.O. Box 22412, Kansas City, MO 64113

For permission to use copyrighted material, grateful acknowledgment
is made to the copyright holders on pages 178-182,
which constitute an extension of this copyright page.

The editors extend special thanks to the late James Dickey and
James Bertolino, who brought to our attention some of the poems collected here;
and to all the poets and artists who donated their work, the publishers and
gallery owners who waived their fees, and to Pat Breed and others
who contributed to this anthology and its mission to help fight hunger.

Cover photograph: Kristen Struebing-Beazley,
Potato on Plant Stand, 1997, polaroid transfer
Book and cover design: Tim Barnhart

Helicon Nine Editions is the publishing arm of the Midwest Center for the
Literary Arts, Inc., a 501 (c) (3) non-profit educational organization,
which receives funding from the National Endowment for the Arts, a federal
agency; the Missouri Arts Council and the Kansas Arts Commission,
state agencies; and individual donors.

Library of Congress Cataloging-in-Publication Data

Spud songs: an anthology of potato poems : to benefit hunger relief / edited by
Gloria Vando and Robert Stewart.
    p. cm.
    ISBN 1–884235–22–0
    1. Potatoes––Poetry. 2. Food habits––Poetry. 3. American poetry––
20th century. I. Vando, Gloria. II. Stewart, Robert.
PS695.P66S68 1999
811' .54080364––dc21   97–42626
                                           CIP

Printed in the United States of America.
HELICON NINE EDITIONS

In a single potato
there are mountains and rivers
—Shinkichi Takahashi
(translated by Lucien Stryk)

Potato Mother, may the potatoes be fat and
plentiful with weeds and stones few and may
they leap into my baskets, yea may they leap
into my sacks, that my weariness at day's end
be rewarded amply, amen.
—Ken Smith, "The Picker's Prayer"
(from a sequence "Casual Labour")

Gertrude Degenhardt.
Ambidextrous, 1998.
Lithograph. 10 copies, 30x26 cm.

CONTENTS

Introduction

Pray for peace and grace and spiritual food,
For wisdom and guidance, for all these are good,
But don't forget the potatoes.

    —J.T. Pettee, "Prayer and Potatoes"

One would be hard pressed to find a food more suited to represent hunger relief than the potato. Food historians claim the Andean tuber, the white potato, will produce more calories per unit of land than any alternative. It is a symbol of both famine and fine cuisine, goodness and gluttony. Its appeal is international, and it comes to us in many flavors: Irish bread, Jewish *latkes*, Italian *gnocchi*, German *Kartoffelklösse*, Greek *kephtides*, Spanish *buñuelos*, French vichysoisse, Swedish *silgratang*, and American hash browns. It is the very spirit of Russia's vodka and Korea's *soju*. Red-blooded American males are said to be "meat-and-potatoes men."

"It is easy to think of potatoes, and fortunately for men who do not have much money, it is easy to think of them with a certain safety," wrote M.F.K. Fisher, sometime between World Wars I and II. "Potatoes are one of the last things to disappear in times of war, which is probably why they should not be forgotten in times of peace."

It could be a measure of the potato's tenacity that the pure, white flesh of it could become, in America, at least, fast or frozen food decked with chili, cheese, bacon bits, and imitation butter; and most children's tastes run solely to chips and fries. Still, for most of us, and certainly for most of the poets represented here, the potato conjures images of family, inner strength, something basic and sustaining, infinitely versatile and, with its own goofy personality, agreeable.

Something central to art, to poetry, is spoken in this collection, as well: that the terms we use to describe ourselves, as humans, are subject to change. Centered around a pivotal being—the character of this book, the potato—each poem contains facets of a star so many sided we can never fully explain its light. Our continued exploration of a single word, of all words, is the journey of the poet; in that journey ordinary things do not remain ordinary. The strength of art is its ability to take something mundane and explode it, to bring change into the world. By focusing on a single object, the poets here take us toward an expanded sense of who we are.

That's the fun of this book. The poet looks into the potato for a new possibility. It's like this: Antoine de Saint Exupery describes a pilot flying over the Andes in a storm, lost; it is not, as he points out, "by piling one adjective upon another" that an author creates drama. The storm loses its importance the more one tries to describe it. "Nothing is dramatic in the world," says Exupery, "nothing pathetic, except in human relations." He calls that the spiritual sense. Only by putting the potato in the context of the spiritual, the human drama, can the writer hope to move people, to change them.

"Let the sky rain potatoes," cries Falstaff in *The Merry Wives of Windsor*, believing them to be an aphrodisiac. Perhaps that explains the names of some varieties—White Rose, Late Beauty of Hebron, Red Bliss. The poetry of the potato lies in how it feeds our dreams, as well as our stomachs.

This is a book with attitude: every poet approaches the potato hungering for something beyond. At its heart, this book acknowledges the contingencies of our lives, chance events, and the empathetic sharing of humanity represented by this single traveler, the potato.

—Robert Stewart and Gloria Vando

Mary S. Watkins.
Heart-shaped Potatoes, 1997.
Photograph.

OPAL WHITELY

TODAY THE GRANDPA DUG POTATOES

Today the grandpa dug potatoes in the field.
I followed along after.
I picked them up and piled them in piles.
Some of them were very plump.
And all the time I was picking up potatoes
I did have conversations with them.
To some potatoes I did tell about
my hospital in the near woods
and all the little folk in it
and how much prayers and songs
and mentholatum helps them to have well feels.

To other potatoes I did talk about my friends—
how the crow, Lars Porsena,
does have a fondness for collecting things,
how Aphrodite, the mother pig, has a fondness
for chocolate creams,
how my dear pig, Peter Paul Rubens, wears a
little bell coming to my cathedral service.

Potatoes are very interesting folks,
I think they must see a lot

of what is going on in the earth.
They have so many eyes.
Too, I did have thinks
of all their growing days
there in the ground,
and all the things they did hear.

And after, I did count the eyes
that every potato did have,
and their numbers were in blessings.

I have thinks these potatoes growing here
did have knowings of star songs.
I have kept watch in the field at night
and I have seen the stars
look kindness down upon them.
And I have walked between the rows of potatoes
and I have watched
the star gleams on their leaves.

—*Adapted by Jane Boulton from Opal's diary, kept at the turn of the century, when she was six years old.*

JANE KENYON

POTATO

In haste one evening while making dinner
I threw away a potato that was spoiled
on one end. The rest would have been

redeemable. In the yellow garbage pail
it became the consort of coffee grounds,
banana skins, carrot peelings.
I pitched it onto the compost
where steaming scraps and leaves
return, like bodies over time, to earth.

When I flipped the fetid layers with a hay
fork to air the pile, the potato turned up
unfailingly, as if to revile me—

looking plumper, firmer, resurrected
instead of disassembling. It seemed to grow
until I might have made shepherd's pie
for a whole hamlet, people who pass the day
dropping trees, pumping gas, pinning
hand-me-down clothes on the line.

WILLIAM MATTHEWS

THIS SPUD'S FOR YOU

1.

Of *solanum tuberosum*, that vagrant vegetable,
the Odysseus of tubers, the lumpy pill of the poor
and starving, the shape-shifting and soothing potato,
I sing. For all the long years it lay locked
in the cool vault of the Andes, above 11,000
feet, where maize won't grow, where the Indians
ate the fattest and best and planted the runts,
so that when the first Europeans held one
it was but a starchy pebble, the Indians
no doubt had a potato song, but the Europeans
brought back to those who had hoped for gold
a mute, misshapen, marble-sized seed crop
and it was reviled. How many times have we met
the news that would save us with contumely?
Thus did Europe greet the immigrant potato.
Not mentioned in the Bible, cousin to nightshade,
it was *flatulent and indigestible . . . , pasty
and naturally insipid; it might prove good to swine.*
It was *an Egyptian fruit whose cultivation
may possibly have some value in the colonies,*
and it was a lurch on the path to hell,

according to Nietzsche: *A diet which consists*
predominantly of rice leads to the use of opium,
just as a diet which consists predominantly
of potatoes leads to the use of liquor.
It was *Ireland's lazy root*, and it ruined
Irish cuisine: *Bread is scarcely ever seen,*
and the oven is unknown. It was, in short,
the durable food of the poor and swarthy,
the bread of vegetables, not scarce, a stay
against famine, bland, despised by the rich.
But in Saxony and Westphalia, 1640,
when all the earth around lay acrid
from twenty-three of the Thirty Years
War, when human and animal corpses lay
swarming with worms, gnawed by birds,
wolves and dogs, for there was nobody
to bury them, pity them or weep for them,
Spanish soldiers arrived with a few potatoes.
When they gave potatoes to the peasants,
these unfortunates began by eating them
just as they were. A little later they planted them.

2.
I sing of Pedro de Cieza de Leon, one
of Pizarro's men, who first among Europeans
sang our rustic root crop in his *Chronicle*
of Peru (1553). And of Sir Francis Drake,

who took unknowingly on board at Cartagena,
in 1586, a few potatoes, and later took on board
in Virginia one Thomas Hariot, who noticed them,
and gave some to John Gerard (his famous *Herball*,
1597, thus misnamed "the Virginia potato").
Did Hariot give some to his boss, Sir Walter
Raleigh, who may then have become first
to plant them in Ireland, on his land
at Youghal, near Cork, late in 1586?
Did Raleigh make a gift to Queen Elizabeth
of some potatoes, and did the befuddled
royal cook discard the tuber and serve
the leaves, tasting like nasty cress?
Of what I do not know I do not sing,
for I have seen what foolish things
many a famous man and fancy writer said
about the potato, and am chastened.

3.
Thus I do not sing Antoine Augustin
Parmentier, the publicist of the potato,
a military pharmacist and pamphleteer,
hero of much Gallic potato lore,
almost all of it wrong, for he did not
charm Marie Antoinette by twining
potato flowers in her hair, nor give
Louis XVI potato flowers for his birthday

(August 23—those would have been wan blooms),
nor did he serve to Benjamin Franklin
a meal in which every course was concocted
from potatoes, though he probably
presided over a like feast once at least.
The tireless potato flak was born to hustle,
that's all, and thus odds were he'd find
later in life a better project than
getting himself noticed by the great
with, as his dull escutcheon, the blunt
lumpy, uningratiating spud. Later
he introduced vaccination against smallpox
in the army, and today his name survives
attached to a soup, a hash and an omelet.

4.
I sing the canny potato, already buried
and thus not burned or trampled by invading
armies. The submarine of the loam,
it bears silently its cargo of carbohydrates
while soldiers and hunters of grouse
and tax assessors conduct important
business overhead. No wonder the poor
love the obdurate tuber, for they share
with it many a survival skill and enemy.
When the knell of the potato blight
rang and rang through starving Ireland,

the potato hunkered down, the lumpy *arriviste*,
blind as a thumb, soft cousin to the stone,
the mineral wealth of the Emerald Isle,
the dull, bland, satisfying food
that Brillat-Savarin proclaimed
only a protection against famine
(only?!), and it spent its three heroisms—
it waited, it grew a little, it flourished—
and the blight was defeated. The plump,
misshapen stowaway, the wily, lumpy
little *pícaro*, the extender of stews
and thickener of soups, the sturdy,
reliable, ugly and invincible potato,
who would not sing this manna among tubers?
We have heard them quoted in this very poem,
and there may be others like them,
though perhaps they are not good singers,
and in any case, you and I, gentle readers,
we can lift our voices. All together now…

JOHN KNOEPFLE

SKIBBEREEN THE FAMINE PIT

it was only that the poor
were driven to the margins
they were the throw away people
their little farms
those fields of rocks in cork and wexford
even less in the townlands

there were caricatures in punch
where have these gone
I could not find them in ireland
nation of twenty year olds
shouting like animals
from the book of kells
when night softens the old streets
dingle or limerick or dublin

everything is completed now
gone back to pasture
all the potatoes shipped in from holland
someone has shut the evil eye
where the famine pits
reach to the bottom of the world

a broad green field here
where my sons could play soccer
and ten thousand
tumbled in one grave here
so many nameless uncarved bones

brickley is here surely
and finn and mccarthy
harrington and driscoll
god keep you from hunger
my great uncles lost here
my keening aunts my cousins

it is the way it is
you were the lesser harvest
once the potato failed
the bloodless sacrifice
when the unexpected bad time came
wrong time famine time

champion and black skerry
those were your favorites
they had the deep eyes

EAVAN BOLAND

THAT THE SCIENCE OF CARTOGRAPHY IS LIMITED

—and not simply by the fact that this shading of
forest cannot show the fragrance of balsam,
the gloom of cypresses
is what I wish to prove.

When you and I were first in love we drove
to the borders of Connacht
and entered a wood there.

Look down you said: *this was once a famine road.*

I looked down at ivy and the scutch grass
rough-cast stone had
disappeared into as you told me
in the second winter of their ordeal, in

1847, when the crop had failed twice,
Relief Committees gave
the starving Irish such roads to build.

Where they died, there the road ended

and ends still and when I take down
the map of this island, it is never so
I can say here is
the masterful, the apt rendering of

the spherical as flat, nor
an ingenious design which persuades a curve
into a plane, but to tell myself again that

the line which says woodland and cries hunger
and gives out among sweet pine and cypress,
and finds no horizon

will not be there.

RAY GONZALEZ

In Peru, the Quechuans Have a Thousand Words for Potato

I hold my cut finger to the ice water,
return from the source of grain in the teeth—
the country where I knew a thousand words for love,

a handful of eye movements, not knowing
which direction to take, which roots to dig
and pile among vegetables.

In Peru, they open their hands,
offer the potato as the fruit from the top of the world,
people who fled the mountains for a crop at lower depths,

descending to cut the potato and find
the white meat, fiber tasting like the grain
that gave them speech.

Their vowels make me wish
I had a thousand words for my body,
a vegetable and tree planted from the testicle,

the black spot in the potato named

for the thousand sons, limbs holding up
the back of the tired worker,

strangers who eat with their fingers and go back
to the high fields for the potato given
the thousand and one name,

dug from the soil they slept on,
the field where they paused to piss
before climbing up the mountain.

ALBERT GOLDBARTH

MISHIPASINGHAN, LUMCHIPAMUDANA, ETC.

Some days, anything is wonderful. In its
detail, in its conception, in its chainlink leading
into the rest of the physical and conceptual cosmos, anything
is wonderful. I'm reading
how the Quechua, in Peru, have a thousand words
for "potato." A thousand! For the new ones
with a skin still as thin as mosquito-wing, for
troll-face ones, for those sneaky burgundy corkscrews
like a devil's dick . . . And there can be
the opposite, yes. There can be a country
with a word like *peynisht*. It's said in a whisper.
Peynisht was the place political prisoners were sent,
a bleak wind-damaged plain, and by a history
of reference, *peynisht* has come to mean
the labor they perform there (for they're sent there yet),
a labor only found in the state-of-being called *peynisht*,
a daily toil without relief of any kind, or hope of pardon,
just this side of unbearable—*peynisht* is that
specific: the labor there, as exactly close to unbearable
as labor can be without crossing fatally over.
There's the sound of wind in the word, a wind with
salt inside that's whipped like spurs across people.

You might think it would be the perfect word
for loose appropriation—so a sour marriage,
a spat-embittered office job, a night of terrible
string-quartet performances in a room so small you
can't scratch . . . the way we use "hellish," these
would be *peynisht*. But it isn't so. It's only
that literal place and the literal spirit-deadening effort
going on there. A man's learned waking on time,
to avoid the clubs. He goes to the pile of stone,
and carries stone, and does nothing but carry stone
in a world without one friend or minute of respite
and when it's dark he returns
to the dirt floor and its shit hole and
they throw him a pan of bad water and a raw potato.
He eats it. And there's only one word.

DENISE LOW

CALIFORNIA POTATOES

The Peruvian restaurant served
everything with lots of rice
and chili sauce. I ordered quinoa
and purple potatoes dotted
with goat cheese, a mounded
plate, steaming, and the potatoes

were firm, as sweet as fruit
but also meaty, meat from a plant,
the strength of rocks and soil
poured into tubers and saved
underground for this moment,

this bite into an apple of the earth,
into the histories of Incan and Irish
and Senegalese and Pakistani—
all the peoples who ate potato
morsels in lamb stew or curry,
peanut soup or chowder or latkes.

Here by the Pacific these Spanish
and Incan people come North

along the coastline, accompanied
by potatoes, like underground fish—
lumpy and slow, inland a few miles,
but always on the move. My fork

presses into white flesh and I taste
all the places potatoes travel
and all their centuries. I smell
the Andes Mountains and coastal
salt-winds, and my stomach fills
with earth, water, and air.

DAVID RAY

WIDOWER

She took such good care of him
that he seldom lifted a finger.
So only now does he stand

by the sink and peel
his first potato, with the paring knife
she left as legacy. The potato,

he notes, fits the human hand,
was made to do so, one
of the miracles. She knew all along.

MICHELLE BOISSEAU

POTATO

I don't want trouble, but the rutabagas
and the turnips, especially the turnips,
are muttering Ingrate, Upstart, and throwing
me looks. Sheez, Louise. I'm hardly escarole.
So I got lots of friends? I'm adaptable,
a hard worker, and I don't ask favors.
Put them in a basket and they're bitter,
put them in a pan, better be copper.
The butter's too pale, the pepper's too coarse.
On and on. With me if I'm forgotten
I turn extrospective and gregarious.
I'm not called the dirt apple for nothing.
I stick my necks out at any warm chink
and grope for the garden on leafy legs.

PETER VIERECK

The Insulted and the Injured
(The Speaker Is a Small Potato Overlooked by All)

I, underground giant, waiting to be fried,
Of all your starers the most many-eyed:
What furtive purpose hatched me long ago
In Indiana or in Idaho?

In Indiana and in Idaho
Earth-apples—deadlier than Eden's—grow,
Puffed up with buried will-to-power unguessed
By all the duped and starch-fed Middle West.

In each Kiwanis Club on every plate,
So bland and health-exuding do I wait
That Indiana never, never knows
How much I envy stars and hate the rose.

You call me dull? A food and not a flower?
Wait! I'll outshine all roses in my hour.
Not wholesomeness but hubris bloats me so
In Indiana and in Idaho.

Something will snap (as all potatoes know)

When—once too often mashed in Idaho—
From my drab husk the shiningest of powers
Rises—
        (I'm sun, I fill the sky)—
                And lours.

RUSH RANKIN

TOURISTS, POTATOES, AND GENOCIDE

A former girlfriend praises my new place
though wonders who the new ashtrays
          are for, so I mumble something
in one direction while glancing
the other way. In one mirror
          I catch her smiling to herself
in another mirror. What frantic lovers
          we were, especially on vacation
in Ireland, where our families began,
where intense people evolve
          backward in order to descend
from themselves. On a parchment map
I brought back the rivers
          of Ireland look like pieces of string.
          As from a satellite passing overhead
we see the blanched ground where
          nothing grew. The ancient path
of English soldiers now shines
like a snail's trail in the moonlit night.
          A loose thread on her sweater
I remove while she searches the map
for some tiny trace of what happened.

Marty Nichols.
Omelette, 1996.
Pastels.

JOSEPH DUEMER

The Best Meals of My Life

When I crack an egg
I usually think
of the French girl
who lived downstairs
in the boarding house
where I endured
the winter following
my first marriage.
She would never
go to bed with me
but showed me instead
in her generosity
how to slip my finger
in a circle inside
the two halves of
a freshly broken
egg shell to extract
the last slick white
to dribble it into
the skillet. Her parents
had lived through
Nazi poverty & she

lectured me—profligate
& depraved—on thrift
& virtue. Out of kindness
she gave me instead
of what I wanted
meals of potatoes
& eggs & that is
the way, isn't it, of virtue
to give not pleasure
but what is necessary
to sustain life: eggs
& potatoes & salt
over which it becomes
possible to talk
& even to think.
Life of the body,
life of the mind.

RODERICK TOWNLEY

THE POTATO

(For LB)

Before the frisk of snow
over Kansas fields, places
of clarity I never knew
I would know—

Before New York, before
the breakup and the break
that drove me from Philly to
"a real job for a change"—

Before the first child,
and the first book, and the first lie—
there was a potato.

O'Henry's it was, nineteen
sixty-nine, a year
before fire gutted it—our table
intimate, our talk
not yet so, the first bravery
of hope between us—

I in black turtleneck,
leather jacket
over the chairback, you
in a not-warm-enough
blue dress. At last:

O'Henry's famous
T-bone and potato, crusty,
top split wide to let
steam out, the melting
butter in. A whiff of it

made us forget wet feet, the war,
winds knifing outside the door. "This
is an incredible potato!"
you cried, and I laughed
because I'd thought the same thing,

and in that moment
everything was clear
between us forever—
until it wasn't anymore.

PAT MORA

ONE POTATO

She buys a potato,
practices cooking
for one.

Home, she scrubs, pierces
the skin, places the sustaining brownness
in the black box, its magic waves.

She sets her place
while her potato softens,
then sits, studies his chair.

She folds her sadness
in clean creases, over
and over, compressing

until it's the size of a pit
she stores inside.
The bell calls her to dinner.

She mashes sour
cream, butter, salt, pepper

into the clouds she feeds herself.

She tastes the altered silence,
bitter and sweet, like plums
that given time, ripen.

TONIGHT

I stand in the kitchen scrubbing
potatoes. A sudden heavy rain
blinds the windows. The door
flies open. A woman, uninvited, rushes in,
stands close to me, says, "remember—
from your Swedish mother you learned
about small white potatoes
boiled, then tossed with butter and dill.
Your French father loved vichysoisse.
You married an Armenian. He
loves rice. Your children learned
to like rice but preferred American
mashed potatoes. You do not know
what they cook now they are grown and
gone, and too many miles keep you apart."

Tonight, in Mexico, I gouge eyes
from small, round, red potatoes,
throw them in a pot of water.
When the water begins to boil,
Mr. Potato Head, abandoned, forgotten
for years, bobs to the top of the pot,

stares with loud, accusing eyes
into mine.
¡Silencio!—I cry—*¡por favor, silencio!*

and slam the lid down on potatoes.

DAN QUISENBERRY

SKINNING

they say the peel is where you get
all the nutrients
but it doesn't taste good even
if you mash in plenty of yellow butter
slabs of thick sour cream
a sprinkle of chives
or rain down lots of pepper and salt
like manna from heaven

come to think of it
i don't eat the peels of most things
not oranges, grapefruits
not mangoes, papayas, lemons
watermelons or cantaloupes
i don't eat the outer peel of onions
or garlic either

i don't like that fuzzy lip skin
on the peach so don't
go throwin' that in there
i've heard one does eat the kumquat
peel and all

but i'm skeptical
won't even touch a raw carrot
yeah get out a knife on that one too
now i've eaten a nectarine
though the skin just rolls up
in my cheeks and gums
and sticks to my teeth

but i do like dissecting
the belly of the hot fat potato
ripe for surgery
bursting forth
with its steaming hot flesh
and when it's nice and mixed
with all those fixin's
i like to scoop the sides
neatly carve it
like i'm makin' a canoe
in some old indian way

and when i'm done
you know i'll hear the
"hey, you didn't eat the skins
that's the best part"
i'll just pat my belly
look at the little canoe
carving and say
"you eat 'em"

DAISY RHAU

POTATOES

The man I love cooks me potatoes,
lifted out from the basement
by good, solid feel.
He shows me what this means
with his hands, open-ended,
fitted for wooden handles
or for the smooth bone of a book.
A bare hand, he tells me,
washes a potato best.

I watch his hands
as he cuts them open,
the uneven pieces bright as soap,
darker underside.
In a year, he's cooked many more
like these, brought up from below,
left rustling in oil.

I have heard of potatoes
that flower in the heat,
burst their skins
into flushed, white tears,

in a way that soil
has everything to do.

Sitting across from him now,
I close my eyes,
turn the warm potato in my mouth,
my tongue quiet with salt.
I could be anywhere, I think,
still this taste I would always know—
Korea, China, Peru.

ROBERT STEWART

Tonight I Thank the Potato

Bare hands wash
a potato best,
the black Andean potato
of the sierra,
potato of year-around spring,
hauled down in sacks
from cloud terraces,
not turned up but fallen,
rain of potatoes
under dense green leaves,
absorbing butter, salt,
the clear light
of broth and cauliflower
and parsnip water.

Hoping for honey,
we achieve the potato,
metabolism of unimagined
slowness. It barely thinks.
Our mother and father
had it tinged in oil,
a little onion and milk—

how the masher clinked
in the family's pot,
muffled,
as if it had one secret
for bread and soup,
a nightshade
of hallucinatory heights.

We never leave behind
the many ways potato
adjusts to our moods,
with peppers
and cheese (forgive us).
It takes from the ladle
a reservoir to hold
not the idea but the gravy.

For centuries we kept it
in cellars and have it
to thank for sanctuary
from tornadoes and
the sun of providence.
Never use a brush
to scrub the back
of a neighbor like this.

Rub between your hands
under a stream,

the blazing skin of pumice,
the stone that forgives
our famines and dehydrations,
potato of our own
short memory,
whose indentation
holds us by the thumb.

ROBERT BLY

A Potato

The potato reminds one of an alert desert stone. And it belongs to a race that writes novels of inspired defeat. The potato does not move on its own, and yet there is some motion in its shape, as if a whirlwind paused, then turned into potato flesh when a ghost spit at it. The skin mottles in parts; potato cities are scattered here and there over the planet. In some places papery flakes lift off, light as fog that lifts from early morning lakes.

Despite all the eyes, we know that little light gets through. Whoever goes inside will find a weighty, meaty thing, both damp and cheerful, obsessive as a bear that keeps swimming across the same river.

When we open our mouth and bite into the raw flesh, both tongue and teeth pause astonished, as a bicyclist leans forward when the wind falls. The teeth say: "I could never have imagined it." The tongue says: "I thought from the cover that there would be a lot of plot…"

SEAMUS HEANEY

DIGGING

Between my finger and my thumb
The squat pen rests; snug as a gun.

Under my window, a clean rasping sound
When the spade sinks into gravelly ground.
My father, digging. I look down

Till his straining rump among the flowerbeds
Bends low, comes up twenty years away
Stooping in rhythm through potato drills
Where he was digging.

The coarse boot nestled on the lug, the shaft
Against the inside knee was levered firmly.
He rooted out tall tops, buried the bright edge deep
To scatter new potatoes that we picked,
Loving their cool hardness in our hands.

By God, the old man could handle a spade.
Just like his old man.

My grandfather cut more turf in a day

Than any other man on Toner's bog.
Once I carried him milk in a bottle
Corked sloppily with paper. He straightened up
To drink it, then fell to right away

Nicking and slicing neatly, heaving sods
Over his shoulder, going down and down
For the good turf. Digging.

The cold smell of potato mould, the squelch and slap
Of soggy peat, the curt cuts of an edge
Through living roots awaken in my head.
But I've no spade to follow men like them.

Between my finger and my thumb
The squat pen rests.
I'll dig with it.

STANLEY PLUMLY

DIGGING POTATOES, 1950

Evenings we went out alone to that long field,
flanked by pasture and a foundry.
The sun would be sitting at one end,
the light almost ankle deep in the dark.
You cursed the shorter days and cooler nights.
Then row by row we laid open the ground,
mingling the one darkness with the other.

Once in a while you helped me lift
a full burlap sack up onto one shoulder
for the slow return to the truck.
Each trip the wet field turned my feet into potatoes.
Usually we finished in a hurry, in air cold enough
I could blow smoke, in order to sit on the tailgate
in the dark drinking beer like old army buddies.

Garry Noland.
Eight Amoeba-like Forms, 1997.
Potato print on Arches.

MARVIN BELL

SOUNDS OF THE RESURRECTED DEAD MAN'S FOOTSTEPS #15

1. One Potato Two

Wrong for the early robin still the potato buries its head in the dirt.
Eyes that cannot see.
1 potato 2 potato a counting game when the choice doesn't matter.
Spotty moisture, overcast, grayness of time immemorial
       they grow in.
Hapless underground severance from light.
Some blight, big bins of why bother if this is the crop you get.
City folk pay big for potato lands.
Acres rank with heavy potato meat.
Fruit of the dirt, bodies bound by gravity.
Face like a potato, chest like a potato, belly like a potato.
Never had a potato a wing.

2. Three Potato Four

All representation is neutral.
Thinking the subject suffered, you suffered.
Bagging the potatoes, you strained a back better suited to crawling.
The worm fitter for tuber life.
Knots in the furrows.

Potato brandy a flat water scraped from the peel.
You are this and these, bulb without light, black hole encrusted.
One's intention to be better than one's roots a betrayal.
Soup and stew, potions to throw cool water on the crop.
Haunted by what it might have been.
In the shadow, a ghost potato where one was taken.

LEATHA KENDRICK

A Simple Thing

Standing at my stove, potatoes to be mashed,
I consider all the years of lumps—
hard white knots awash in gluey pots.
My mother taught high school home ec,
but didn't tell me how to do it right.
Did I ever ask?

"Leave your Irish whites drying in the pot;
make sure they're riced before you put in milk"—
someone's instruction rises through my head.
The dry part I know from my husband's aunt
but "riced" is not her word, or one of mine—
a cooking term, something my mother might
have said—though she never told me, I am sure.
Never acted like I needed to know,
me with my books and
better things to do.
Maybe she only hoped.

It wasn't something I thought must be learned—
a simple thing
like mashed potatoes. Marriage with its mass

of simple things that everybody knows.
"I'll tell my daughters all the tricks,"
I think. One of them sits behind me
at the table with her book,
chores completed, waiting for this food—
a plain meal of meat and beans,
that with these knotted roots
gathers itself simply
toward our plates, its mysteries
safe inside our silence.

Done, whole and skinless, white
tubers resting in the pot
shatter at my thrust
to powdery piles—without glue,
no accusing lumps.
Ready to take up the liquid.
A girl, eleven and innocent
of potato mashing—
I leave her be.
These spuds stir up smooth and buttered,
heavy, white with milk. When she's ready
she'll find what she needs.

I turn. "Call your sisters down to supper"
is all she'll hear me say.

PHILIP MILLER

Peeling Potatoes

In the kitchen
everything looked worn:
dented kettle,
black bottomed pans,
chipped enamel sink
knives honed to skewers,
teaspoons thinning,
breadboard, rolling pin,
smooth as driftwood,
and Grandmother,
bent and drawn
as she peeled
a bowl of russets
in the half-light,
spilled shadows everywhere
darkened edges and corners
charcoaled the outlines
of each stool and cupboard,
of Grandmother's face,
hollowing her cheeks,
leaving her sharp violet eyes
pin points

as she looked up
a second, gazed through
the window,
staring hard
at the old winter moon.

S. B. SOWBEL

"If You're Lost"

a renowned interpreter of
the stars once said:

"Listen, you know I work with the sky
and it has taught me much
about place and planets, even ours.

So if you want to feel
your feet on this earth,
to stay grounded,
to remind yourself
exactly where you are

get a potato, that's right
a potato. Put it
in your pocket
and think of it

down deep in the dirt
some odd, rotten chunk
of a modest dinner, discarded;
a rough-skinned stone

with nourishing innards
turning itself
year after year
by sheer memory
and not a little magic
into a full future
much like its pre-prandial pasts
with a promise of more dinners
and more discardings;
a finer library
than fancy references
or phone books
for life at a forgotten address."

for Isabeth Hardy and Alice O. Howell

MICHAEL DENNIS BROWNE

Two: Inhale and raise the arms. Bend backward

You, I accuse.
You, Michael Moon.

Mad Moon Boy.
How mad you are, nobody knows.

You get drunk at dawn.
You ride the spider bareback across the dawn.

You stand on your head on the moon,
alone. Little Tomb Lover.
Ophelia, Ophelia, drifting along;
ah, such a sad song!

When you were small,
what was your nightmare?
My nightmare was
that the moon rose over the world's edge;
it stared at me; it climbed, it smiled,
and was mocking me.
If I didn't wake myself up
before it climbed too high.
I'd be dead.

What now do you dream?
I feel the shadows of Europe creep
over my sheets.
I hear the French,
I hear Agincourt and its arrows.

I see my brain,
my brain the potato,
the black three-pound potato
in an Irish field.
I hold up my brain,
caked with the dirt of ancestors,
I wave it—
do all my thoughts
come from this thing?

I rinse it in a stream
like an old washerwoman,
I race through the streets,
this moon-brain in my hands.

Eli, Eli, lama sabachthani?

This is the night the dead headmaster
turns toward you with a fresh exam,
this is the night the crucifix clicks open
under the black gloves of the burglar.

This is the night the rat runs out
for his free gift,
this is the night
the boneless bird
flies.

This is the night the children
crouch in the stone rocket,
this is the night a mother chains
her child to a dead animal.

Eddie, Eddie...

O you Moon,
you Potato Man,
you Toy—
how can we rid the town of this rat?

Moon, I summon you.
Michael Moon, I call you out
from your shallow grave,

from your brown bag
in the Potter's Field—come forth.
"Moon get up and mend your wounds—"
all the children know *that* song.

See, the rocking chair rocks backwards and forwards,

trying to rock itself into a man—
"Moon get up and mend your wounds—"
See, the woman croons a quiet song
to the driftwood she holds in her arms.

Moon,
Michael Moon,
mend yourself,
come forth.

                    —*from Sun Exercises*

Eli, Eli, lama sabachthani?: My God, my God, why hast Thou forsaken me?

ARTHUR SZE

THE DAY CAN BECOME A ZEN GARDEN OF RAKED SAND

The day can become a Zen garden of raked sand
or a yellow tanager singing on a branch;

feel the terrors and pleasures of the morning:
in Tianjin all the foreigners are sent to a movie

and they must guess at what the authorities
do not wish them to see; dream a rainy landscape:

the Jemez Mountains breaking up in mist and jagged light
into a series of smaller but dazzling ranges;

to distinguish the smell of calendula from delphinium
is of no apparent consequence, but guess that

crucial moments in history involve an unobtrusive
point flaring into a startling revelation;

now be alive to the flowering chives by the window;
feel the potato plant in the whiskey barrel soak up sun;

feel this riparian light,
this flow where no word no water is.

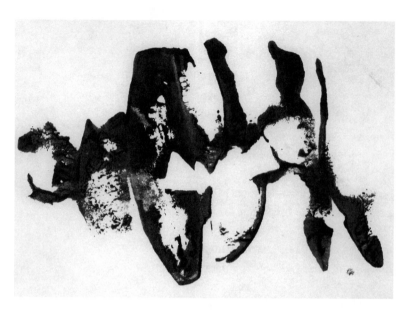

Shea Gordon.
Dead Sea, 1997.
Potato print on construction paper.

THOMAS ZVI WILSON

ALICE POTATO

Solanum tuberosum:
a Talmudic study

for the French

Pomme de terre:
apple of the eye
and earth.

for her

But for fur a winter groundhog,
she swells from seed
to bear tubers.

for us

Fingernails scrape earth's skin.
We lift Alice to our world
to carve her, eat her,
practice a craft or plant her.

for him

Seamless like a mermaid,
white inside with colored skin,
she fills his mind the way
she fits his open hand.

for the record

Imperfect sphere
curls into self,
must rot to resurrect.

MALCOLM GLASS

RISKS

You know the risks when you work
in potatoes, all those eyes, tough
and cynical, accusing you of loftiness.

The digging machine plunders the dense
fruit of the earth and conveys them
up the ramp to pour them into the truck.
Maybe you see a landslide of rocks
sweeping down a dry riverbed
and over the edge of a dead
waterfall. Or perhaps you see yourself
driving a deserted road in swamp country
some morning at two-thirty, straight
into the heart of a storm
of hail big as baseballs.

                   The potatoes come
from their bath (clean ones bring a higher
price) and roll down the chute, numbly
bumping each other along, like somnolent
sheep, like a river which tells you

the sun is falling (it doesn't matter
which way).

       You know beyond admission
that sooner, later, the potatoes, or another
agency appointed by physics, will take you:

One morning as you work on your farm
in Wiggins, Colorado, trying
to remember the vibrant mouth
of the dusky-skinned brunette
in your dream, a joist above you
cracks, the floor of the warehouse loft
gives way, and several tons
of potatoes descend
to bury you.

GLORIA VANDO

ON HEARING THAT A POTATO COSTS $70 IN SARAJEVO

in memory of SPUD: Society for the Prevention of Unhealthy Diets

Potato: for want of it the Irish invaded Boston,
Suffolk County, maybe even Maine, before
settling into a life of slim-trim resignation,
replicating hometown farms, starch swelling
the landscape in mounds the shape of potatoes—
did they in fact make it to Idaho, or was that
another hungry invasion, or was it coincidence,
the commonwealth of cuisine?—no matter,
they would always be paired with that symbol
of nagging contradictions served up in dual images
of gluttony and starvation, frailty and pollution
(the first insecticide having been invented
to prevent the blight of the potato beetle—
a contradiction in itself, with its black and yellow
stripes camouflaging a pin-prick of a mouth
that would devour whole undersides of leaves in
picoseconds, and its equally disarming orange-yellow
eggs clustered like tiny land mines set to explode
at deadly intervals—and just this morning
I was reading a loud black and yellow *WARNING!*
about its pesticidal progeny: *this* -zine and *that* -zine

poisoning our mid-western streams, our drinking
water, our *children*, for godssake—leaving nothing
for us to do but move back to Boston, Suffolk
County, and points east); potato as victim and
victimizer, like the Irish themselves, trapped
in the Belfast of the human condition, the torn
war zone of the heart, a people whose namesake
is the jig, the wake, and the potato, the *Irish* potato—
even though its zigzag journey started in Peru,
crossing the Atlantic in the deep hull of Spanish
shame, where some poor slob of a galley slave
found himself *jodido* through centuries of KP;
even though all of Europe thrived on it through
two world wars, and the neutral nations of Benelux
(*Nazis? where? where?*) craved it and carved it
on their plates with gusto and a kind of reverence
for its neutral flavor—I know this first-hand,
the rest I read in the third or fourth edition
of the *Columbia Encyclopedia*, which I cross-
referenced with my late friend Eddy Iino,
while feasting on burgers and french fries,
soon after I returned from Amsterdam, where
my schoolmate Denise, a hefty ballerina, once
invited me to dinner, a pleasant surprise since
the Dutch were still listing from the unexpected
Nazi wallop and some said her father was ill,
the SS screaming nightly obscenities in his dreams,

so ill he'd had to resign from the University—
foolish, weak man, they said, the war was over, *over*,
you had to get on with your life, wear your
shirtsleeves long, tightly buttoned at the wrist,
never, *never* view your body in the mirror, that's
what any sane person would do, they said—
and that evening the Delft china and sterling were
laid out for Denise's friend, crystal water goblets
reflecting the pink and purple petals of the tulips
from my garden, and Mrs. van Beek, in a demure
v-necked navy blue dress, nodded and smiled
at me, her first guest since World War II, and
gently—oh so gently—doled out helping after
helping of unaccompanied peeled, boiled, and
quartered potatoes—*a tuber sonata!*—while
the rest of us (carefully skirting van Gogh),
discussed deStijl, Pater, Piet Mondrian, and—
Oh yes, Professor van Beek asked, *have you seen
the queen's photograph in the paper?*—Wilhelmina
sloshing heroically through flood waters of the low
lowlands, the soggy weight of her hem revealing
the residue of nightshade on her regal buttocks—
*and did you hear Prince Bernhardt extolling the virtues
of Volendam on the radio?*—his actual words now
muffled by the enduring properties of starch
gluing my host's tongue to the roof of his mouth
so that Prince Bernhardt, hero though he was,

produced merely an inarticulate phlegmy growl—
nngkhggnngchgnnngggrrachkkrchrecggrr—a jarring
characteristic of Dutch, with or without
potatoes—*aardappelen*—earth's apples (as opposed
to heaven's, where Spanish jokes about *la papa*,
el Papa, and *papá* would never circulate)—
earth's apples, wearing a dull and dirty post-
Edenic coat, this time, to help poor Adam ("man"
in Hebrew) resist temptation: there's just no biting
into a raw potato; it's got to be peeled, cooked,
blinded—thereby affording Adam an unobserved
hour or two to think things over: the potato, not
unlike an unloaded gun by the bed or an unhoned
knife in the kitchen, gives one pause, a chance
to look around, reflect, choose one's arena
with care: a woman, they say, kills in the kitchen
(a sharp blade to his gut), a man in the bed (twisted
linens knotted at her throat), but in other rooms
of the human house, where bare hands reign,
our only recourse is to put ours together and pray
for a deterrent—a sudden surge of arthritis or
peripheral neuropathy or impotence, any of which
can be suppressed with megadoses of minerals,
abundant in the skins of the coveted, ubiquitous,
though sometimes unaffordable potato.

---

jodido—"screwed"   *la papa*—the potato
el Papa—the Pope   *papá*—daddy

PETER COOLEY

Van Gogh's *The Potato Eaters*

Not ever to sit down, a part of one another
in the old way this hunger takes for granted—
this is how we stand, the woman thinks.

Not ever to be apart from one another
the man thinks, at the altar of the table,
the potatoes almost weightless on our tongues.

And the tea—let me speak—in thick, bone mugs
consuming them entirely until, risen,
their spirits can be thanksgiving's scrawny ghost.

Without him, she tastes this to herself, shakes on more salt.
Without her, he savors it, with other women.
And the bastings, might, could, seal in the precious juice.

They prepare a feast at the table of each other.
They sit down, bowed in silence, tooth and claw
ruddy at the unspoken, ravening.

JOYCE CAROL OATES

IN JANA'S GARDEN

—for Jana Harris

Here, in July, in Jana's weedy garden,
heat rising from the earth like vapor
and such luxuries of vegetables!—
red onions and parsley and peppers and
beets and mint and lettuce newly bolted
thigh-high and sweet corn in tall shaggy
rows and potatoes unearthed like crude
gems heaped in our arms—and thank you,
thank you for every gift this life we
haven't deserved and now at harvest,
when the air pulses with heat and the sky
is massed with fat dimpled clouds like pride
licking itself unrepentant, hungry
for all you can give.

DAVID WILLIAMS

In Praise of the Potato

Potato, sojourner north, first sprung
from the flanks of volcanos, plainspoken kin

to bright chili and deadly nightshade,
sleek eggplant and hairy tobacco,

we could live on you alone if we had to,
and scorched-earth marauders never bothered you much.

I love you because your body's a stem,
your eyes sprout, and you're not in the Bible,

and if we did not eat your strength,
you'd drive it up, into a flower.

EAMON GRENNAN

POTATOES

(for Peter Russell)

Neglected for days, for weeks,
I love how these old potatoes grow in the dark
in their earthy jackets: the way

pale tubers curl and clutch, become
clusterings of white hair or a seaweed tangle
with designs on life. It's their silence,

how life moves simply through them,
how they contain and overspill with it,
something desperate but deliberate

about their clear if fragile sense of a future
which, if it's to come to pass,
they have to be halved or quartered

and buried somewhere, this severing and going down
being the only way—if you want
fullness, a field dark green and petalled with

white silk in the wind in late summer
when already the days, warm as they are,
have started to turn, growing shorter.

RICHARD WILBUR

POTATO

for André du Bouchet

An underground grower, blind and a common brown;
Got a misshapen look, it's nudged where it could;
Simple as soil yet crowded as earth with all.

Cut open raw, it looses a cool clean stench,
Mineral acid seeping from pores of prest meal;
It is like breaching a strangely refreshing tomb:

Therein the taste of first stones, the hands of dead slaves,
Waters men drank in the earliest frightful woods,
Flint chips, and peat, and the cinders of buried camps.

Scrubbed under faucet water the planet skin
Polishes yellow, but tears to the plain insides;
Parching, the white's blue-hearted like hungry hands.

All of the cold dark kitchens, and war-frozen gray
Evening at window; I remember so many
Peeling potatoes quietly into chipt pails.

"It was potatoes saved us, they kept us alive."
Then they had something to say akin to praise
For the mean earth-apples, too common to cherish or steal.

Times being hard, the Sikh and the Senegalese,
Hobo and Okie, the body of Jesus the Jew,
Vestigial virtues, are eaten; we shall survive.

What has not lost its savor shall hold us up,
And we are praising what saves us, what fills the need.
(Soon there'll be packets again, with Algerian fruits.)

Oh, it will not bear polish, the ancient potato,
Needn't be nourished by Caesars, will blow anywhere,
Hidden by nature, counted-on, stubborn and blind.

You may have noticed the bush that it pushes to air,
Comical-delicate, sometimes with second-rate flowers
Awkward and milky and beautiful only to hunger.

DENISE LEVERTOV

ROASTING POTATOES

Before the Wholesale Produce Market
moved to the Bronx, what wild
Arabian scenes there'd be each night
across from our 5th floor window—
the trucks arriving from all over
as if at a caravanserai under the weird
orange-bright streetlights
(or was it the canvas awnings that were orange,
sheltering the carrots, the actual oranges. . .).
Great mounds of fruit, mountain ranges
of vegetables spread in the stalls, and now
more unloading, and the retail trucks
rolling up to bargain and buy till dawn. . . .
Unemployed men, casual labor, hung around,
waiting for clean-up jobs; some were glad
to get some bruised produce if no work.
And the Catholic Worker pickup
came by at the last,
for anything unsold, unsaleable (but not
uncookable).   In the '60s
there was the Bowery, yes, and ordinary
urban winos, but not

throngs of homeless men
and hardly ever a homeless woman except
for those you'd see down at Maryhouse or sometimes,
(conspicuous, embarrassing) in the waiting room at Grand Central.
There were men, though, among those frequenting the market,
who clearly had no fixed abode; we thought of them
as old fashioned hobos.
Some time in the night, or weekends
when the big parking lot, the whole
commercial neighborhood (vanished now), was deserted,
they'd build fires in old metal barrels
and sit round them on upturned crates
roasting fallen potatoes they'd salvaged,
(a regular feast, once when a truck
lost its load) and talking, telling stories,
passing a bottle if they had one.
The war was (remotely) gearing up,
Vietnam a still unfamiliar name,
the men were down on their luck,
some White, some Black, not noticeably hostile,
most of them probably drunks:
you couldn't call it
a Golden Age; and yet
around those fires, those roasting potatoes,
you could see, even from our top-storey windows,
not even down there catching the smoky
potato-skin smell or hearing
fragments of talk and laughter—*something*

—you name it, if you know, I can't. . .
something you might call blesséd? Is that hyperbole? Something kind?
Something not to be found in the '90s, anyway.
Something it seems we'll have to enter the next millennium
lacking, and for the young,

                      unknown to memory.

H. L. HIX

MAN IN NOVOSIBIRSK

Leaning into the handlebars,
he pushes his bike up the path
to the center of Russia. Scars
connect his private Irkutsk with
Moscow across a birthmark broad
as the taiga. Balancing bags
of potatoes resurrected
from their fifteen-feet-deep grave dug
by younger arms and a younger
back, he prepares for the harshness
of beauty: more die of hunger
in the bright weather before crops
than starve in snow. Not much farther,
another man gathers mushrooms.

X. J. KENNEDY

DIRTY ENGLISH POTATOES

Baildon, West Yorkshire

Steam-cleaned, so groundless you'd believe
   Them exhaled from some passing cloud,
The Idahoes and Maines arrive
   Same-sized, tied in their plastic shroud.

Their British kindred, unconfined,
   Differ in breeding, taste, and size.
They come with stones you mustn't mind.
   You have to dredge their claypit eyes.

Their brows look wrinkled with unease
   Like chilblain-sufferers in March.
No sanitized machines are these
   For changing sunlight into starch—

Yet the new world's impatient taint
   Sticks to my bones. I can't resist
Cursing my mucked-up sink. I want
   Unreal meals risen from sheer mist.

JOHN HOLLANDER

COMMENT ON AN OBSERVATION BY ONE OF MY MASTERS

> *In all the good Greek of Plato*
> *I lack my roastbeef and potato*
> —John Crowe Ransom

But that's because back in the time of Plato
No *nous* could grab the form of The Potato,

Nor would you find pommes frites nor yet potato
Latkes at dinner chez censorious Cato

(Although *Kartoffelsalat*—at some NATO
Power lunch, would feature the potato.)

I knew a wretched soul who lived at eight-o-
Eight Gloom Road who hated the potato

In any form—but there are those who know some
Great ways to cook solanum tuberosum

And as for me, but that I watch my weight, O
Childish delight, I'd live on mashed potato!

(Yet no such love, but questions of belief
Choke discourse on the matter of roast beef.)

OTTO PIENE

The Prussian king, Frederick the Great, introduced potatoes to German agriculture. He was a Francophile: spoke mostly French and made Voltaire, among other French luminaries, an artist-in-residence at his court, Sanssouci, in Potsdam. The two frequently exchanged bons mots and what we would now call *poemes objets*. (Jeu de Paume, at the corner of the Tuileries in Paris, is now a contemporary art museum; it was formerly an interior ball court.) The translation follows:

F: *Venez à sous p à cent sous six!* (*Venez à souper à Sanssouci!* Come to supper at Sans Souci!)

V: *J grand a petit—* (*J'ai grand appetit—pommes français?* I have a big appetite— French potatoes?)

F: (*Pommes prussiens!* Prussian potatoes!)

MAXINE CHERNOFF

BREASTS

If I were French, I'd write
about breasts, structuralist treatments
of breasts, deconstructionist breasts,
Gertrude Stein's breasts in Père-Lachaise
under stately marble. Film noire breasts
no larger than olives, Edith Piaf's breasts
shadowed under a song, mad breasts raving
in the bird market on Sunday.
Tanguy breasts softening the landscape,
the politics of nipples (we're all equal).
A friend remembers nursing,
his twin a menacing blur. But wait,
we're in America, where breasts
were pointy until 1968. I once invented
a Busby Berkeley musical with naked women
underwater sitting at a counter
where David Bowie soda-jerked them
ice cream glaciers. It sounds so sexual
but had a Platonic airbrushed air.
Beckett calls them dugs, which makes me think
of potatoes, but who calls breasts potatoes?

Bolshoi dancers strap down their breasts
while practicing at the bar.
You guess they're thinking of sailing,
but probably it's bread, dinner,
and the Igor Zlotik Show (their
Phil Donahue). There's a photo of me
getting dressed where I'm surprised
by Paul and try to hide my breasts, and another
this year, posed on a pier, with my breasts
reflected in silver sunglasses. I blame
it on summer when flowers overcome gardens
and breasts point at the stars. Cats
have eight of them, and Colette tells
of a cat nursing its young while
being nursed by its mother. Imagine the scene
rendered human. And then there's the Russian
story about the woman...but wait,
they've turned the lights down, and Humphrey
Bogart is staring at Lauren Bacall's breasts
as if they might start speaking.

PRINCESS

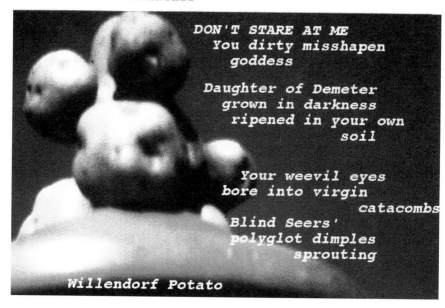

DON'T STARE AT ME
You dirty misshapen
goddess

Daughter of Demeter
grown in darkness
ripened in your own
soil

Your weevil eyes
bore into virgin
catacombs
Blind Seers'
polyglot dimples
sprouting

Willendorf Potato

One of Henry's garden variety sculptures
   Turned up moribund princess
(She only dines on mashed potatoes)

eyes popping
cancers
 breasts
raw tubers
(more's a comin')

My peeler guts
one of those raw
           seer's eyes

potato fumes rise

fresh wax slides

against my fingers

I'm happy not to see.

ELISE PASCHEN

POTATOES CORIANDER

For John Fuller (on his sixtieth birthday)

Harbored inside a much-thumbed *Joy of Cooking*,
A scrap of paper, brown ink scrawled on top—
Potatoes Coriander a.k.a.
Potatoes à la John—what he invented
Years (seems like months) ago at Magdalen, Oxford.

Bud-tantalizing: garlic, ginger, mustard-seed,
Ingredients and steps once spelled out, now
Rarely repeated. How could I presume?
Trying to cook is like scaling Parnassus.
Here's my translation (a short cut) which I concoct
Devotedly: Boil the potatoes. Drain.
Add butter, coriander powder (Spice Islands).
Yield: two servings…plus souvenirs of **JOHN**!

ROBERT PETERS

POTATOES

You eat whatever you can.
After a point you give up the search
for fresh red endive, artichokes,
avocados.
You unearth potatoes, again, by hand,
by the same hand that isolates the self,
and removes the fruit;
the vine undisturbed,
the root system kept intact,
white tubers never missed,
white tubers to keep one sane.

Nam June Paik.
Couch Potato, 1994.
2 KEC 9" televisions model 9BND, 1 Samsung 19" television, 3 Samsung 13"
televisions, reclining chair, 2 mailboxes, computer monitor casing and keyboard,
2 computer keyboards, 2 Spectron datascopes, 3 metal cabinets, neon, 2 laser disk
players, 2 original Paik laser disks, 74x67x91 inches.

DINA VON ZWECK

ONE MAN'S POTATO CHIP

History repeats a work of
art. After Bill Gates installed
the Potato Chip in every
computer, skies became cluttered.

Hackers got a glimpse of things
before anyone had actually
seen them. Navigators found
an interesting number of infinite objects.

Life became an all-night travel
agency. Little gray light now
sparkled. Screens were brimmed
with wonders, like the ghosts of dead poets.

CRASH! When I say "history repeats
a work of art," I'm thinking of
de Kooning's *Woman*, and how fiercely
she brings all communication to a standstill.

When the Potato Chip fails and
the world's computers crash together,
we are left with silence—and
She, the wild brushstroke. A visionary desire.

LEQUITA VANCE-WATKINS

PASSACAGLIA

for David Alpher

Potato, you thunder along
your ground bass
underground in three-quarter time.

Off to the north sweet notes
of peas and corn come alive,
rattling vines of squash
take up the line,
the watermelon wait.

Even Dido knew you were King
when in Purcell purity
asked remembrance
                    When I am laid in earth
a place you have known on shifting continents
for a baritone of years.

COLETTE INEZ

DIGGING POTATOES

Idaho Russets, Late Beauties of Hebron
kidnapped and hauled
past corrugated fields,

in the market they sing gospels.
Once I dug up spuds in the forties,
two bits an hour for summer work.

I never heard the produce sing.
But heaped up in bins
these tubers croon as I lean down

to better hear: "Abide With Me"
and "A-Rock-a My Soul."
God knows, I scorched their skins,

scooped out the flesh,
myself, a bon vivant, glutted
with baco bits, butter and salt.

MADELINE DEFREES

Variations on the Edible Tuber

Your potatoes are affected with a condition known as hollow heart. It is not a disease and cannot be transmitted but is due to growing conditions.

Hollow heart can be caused by too much moisture, or too much variation in soil moisture—too dry one week and too wet the next—or simply by insufficient farmyard or bulky compost in the soil.

—M.V. CHESNUT

1

The thing I hate most is eating
potatoes
with a hollow heart: it is not
that they communicate regret to the palate,
nor yet the tongue's bland burden
of what is mealy and missing. It is not
disease they transmit. Their state is due to growing
conditions that affect the night-
shade family.
My potatoes are affected. I eat them
with a hollow heart
inert before extremes. I would like to drop
the hot potato if it were not
too late. Perhaps my mouth will water
by spring, my dreams fill
with sweet potatoes (which see).

2

The eyes of potatoes are on me.
I become what I eat.
I am one of the fighting Irish with a white
hollow heart and discrete
conditions. Down with potatoes! We revert
to the deadly nightshade.
Thrive underground in the panhandle.
turn Idaho red.

3

Belladonna!
I remember how the head of purple flowers
became you! Your soothing
dark fruit. You introduced me to the mainland.
Your Anti-Spasmodic properties,
all your respectable cousins en route:
Tomato, Pepper, Tobacco. You favored
the rococo Potato, dangled the Jimsonweed branch
from the darkest part
of your family tree though the Weedgrower's Annual
traced its ancestry to Jamestown,
to Atropos, one of the Three
Wide-Eyed Fates who enlarge
their pupils.

4

Now we come back to the potato-bore
in polite circles
shacked up with the more orthodox nema-
tode. In British Columbia where I run a small
tenant farm at the end of the road
we call ourselves spuds—the people's friend—
our Yankee disease
limp as our fried French. We scheme
to get by on starch and staples
not much Canadian beef.
We are kept under quarantine,
transported by rail,
fleshy parts hawked: the high cost
of living for sale
in the public market.

5

Dear Potato Doctor, old Chesnut, you said
this is not a disease
you would recommend
no cure, though you implied a remedy of sorts:
manure or bulky compost
to create
more even
conditions...

Of late I have followed your Recycled Matter Diet
but I am whipped potatoes, beaten—
too watery or too dry—
my hollow disguise served up on a platter,
eaten. Surely an old potato lover
versed in his art
can sprout a thin hope of remission
even if I am not sick. How about a ground cover?
I dream that the emptiness swells
to my peeling.
Doctor, you must recognize this heart
condition however extreme
this new feeling.

SUSAN WHITMORE

OUTSIDE

wind whips red
and orange against window glass.
The doctor says, Inoperable.

My friend V. Lies scattered,
dusty leaves across the fissured earth
of hospital bed.

Blind as an eye without an iris,
a tumor fists itself in her left lung, growing
a round white body all its own.

V. swallows, opens palms on autumn's blaze.
The fruited root will not be taken
without killing her winding stem,

flower memory, fleshy green.

ROCHELLE RATNER

The Potato

The potato is on the dishrack
The washable pyrex frypan is in the closet
The dog is outside

*

The potato is being cut into slices
The knife moves leisurely from right to left,
enhanced by the efforts of sunlight
The last slice appears somewhat different

*

The potato is baked in a wine sauce
The child stares at it angrily,
stuffing his mouth with the warm flesh of a cow

The potato grows cold, giving off a faint gold light
The candles are still in their boxes

The child takes down one box, opens it,
and twists the wax rhythmically thru his fingers
He seems to be very contented

*

The potato is in a jar on the windowsill
You have been watering it faithfully every day

On warm days the window is open
Sparrows perch on the rim of the jar,
taking proud sips from the water
Some stay there longer than others.

MARTÍN ESPADA

PITCHING THE POTATOES

My father was a semipro pitcher in the city,
with a curveball that swooped
like a sea gull feeding at the dump.
One day he slipped on infield grass
and heard his shoulder crunch.
Still, pitching to me years later,
his curveball would sometimes tease
my clutching mitt, and thump my chest.

My younger brother wouldn't eat the mashed potatoes.
I smirked, belly pregnant with tubers,
a drowsy toad full of dragonflies. My brother's potatoes
would soon slide down my amphibian gullet.

But my father's jaw was quivering: "You won't eat, hah?"
Then the plate of mashed potatoes
sailed over my brother's bristling crewcut head,
splattered and pasted itself to the wall,
a white oval staring at us from the white plaster
like minimalist art.

My toad eyes strained alertly.

That wasn't the curveball.
My mother bowed her head, another silent prayer,
though I think God was listening to thunderstorms in the Amazon.
The plate began to slide down the wall.
Later, my mother sponged the mashed potatoes away.
I wanted to lick the sponge.

My mother still prays today; she is patient with God.
My brother is a vegetarian.
My father says the Giants have no pitching.
In my sleep, I duck beneath a plate of mashed potatoes
orbiting my head, like a fake flying saucer
suspended by wire
in a snapshot from thirty years ago.

ROBLEY WILSON

A POTATO ESCAPE

When I was fifteen I stood
before the showcase in
Shaw's Hardware and asked
Mister Shaw to put aside
that .25-calibre Beretta
pistol on the bottom shelf.
I had twelve dollars, earned
on my paper route. I'd have
the thirty-dollar balance
by Labor Day.

                  I'd aimed it
more than once: blued-steel
barrel, pearl handle cool
in my grip, small enough
to conceal from anyone—
Don't ask me: why on earth
did a fifteen year old need
a weapon? This was America,
the nineteen-forties, let's
not pretend a crime rate

out of hand. I wanted a gun—
no reason, only desire.

What happened? Mister Shaw
called up my father, turned
me in. My father scolded,
read me an angry riot act,
put the kibosh on the deal.
He made me bank my money.
What fancy did he rob me of?
What did I know back then
about fathers and sons,
what they contest for?

One Sunday in the comics
a Dick Tracy villain—was it
the Brow?—broke jail.
He'd stolen from the mess
a raw potato, carved it
in the shape of a pistol,
and from the infirmary
he'd smuggled the iodine
that colors starch blue-
black. The guard was fooled
by the potato that looked
like a gun.

Now you know:
fifteen, I was prisoner
in a juvenile hall; I had
to make a break for it,
elude my turnkey parents,
become my own man. I saw
myself, like Brow, pacing
the narrow cell of my room—
my thoughts dark, my plan
secret, my mind rehearsing
words to go with the deed:

Be wary, my dear mother.
If I should volunteer
to peel potatoes, mash them
smooth as buttered silk,
how will you know I've not
kept back one wise-eyed
Idaho, carved my Beretta,
tinctured it and run off—
your baby boy grown up,
at large, and (oh!) a risk
to all the future world?

THOMAS MICHAEL MCDADE

THE POTATOES OF THE FIELD

Boone understands
how tough it would be
to steal them now.
Lean too close,
an alarm sounds
like angry jays.
And guards with rubber soles
that tweet on the hardwood
don't nap like those at Marmottan
where Monets are easy.
But casing the Unicorn Tapestries
at the Cloisters is a gas.
In the captivity scene there are 85
plants to identify.
There are gorgeous guides
who look Boone in the eye
and softly suggest he imagine
the intensity of the colors back then.
He does and winks.
Then whispers,
"Looks like Groucho Marx,"
to puzzled children

searching for the hidden face
in the fountain tapestry—
legend says it's the weaver's.
But Boone's biggest kick
is rich-looking folks
who grow pale
upon learning French peasants
claimed the carpets
during the Revolution,
to use in fields
to shelter spuds.
A tale that gives Boone hope
and a shiver.

WALTER BARGEN

POTATO CONFLICTS

1   Unsung Spud Fights Axis Powers

In the captured photo album, attic-dusted and insect-infested,
a smiling nameless face appears in regimental formation;
smiling as he practiced throwing a grenade nicknamed
a potato masher, and two broad smiles fill the next frame
as he exposed the shrapnel wound of his friend from
the accident; he's smiling from under his helmet
as he paddled across a winter river; and in the smoky
room crowded with too many drunken faces smiling
with sentimental songs; but then I see it in a yellowed
photograph on the final page, a potato disguised as
the Graf Zeppelin, dumping ballast on his bespeckled face.

2   Cannon Fodder

All that's needed is three or four feet of plastic pipe,
one end capped closed, the other left a speechless "O,"
a small hole just above the cap that can be securely
covered, an aerosol can of starter ether left over
from winter engine troubles, a butane lighter set

for high flame, and perhaps a palisade of cottonwoods
along a steep bank, and a few beers, or more than
a few beers, and then it's time to defend the river
from behemoth barges that traffic slowly past,
so from the grocery bag pick a right-diameter
potato and force it tight into the pipe, prime
the hole with ether and ignite it. The potato goes
ballistic for three or four hundred feet before
ringing the steel hull or falling into the murky
current and turning to catfish fodder.

3   Garden Casualties

Green spring and I'm racing through intersections
of rain and time.

Up the row, down the row, under the row—
eyes in all directions.

But what mortal collisions;
boiled! mashed! fried!

What to expect?
Crossing without looking

in both directions: up, down.
Blind as a root, dumb as a tuber.

Jan Gilbert.
Four French Fries, 1997.
Mixed Media.

DENNIS BERNSTEIN

DREAMING OF FRENCH FRIES BEHIND THE PROJECTS IN FAR ROCKAWAY

The black bitch cat scratched the rat's jelly-brain clean
from the gray half-moon of its skull. A few yards away, jo jo
played with a red pickup truck that his mind was driving across
country to a state called California where his mother served
french fries to red- and white-faced surfers.

The cat finished lunch and was rough-tonguing his raggy
paws. The white sun burned an eye into noon. jojo felt the
moist heat at the crown of his head like a hand, like the barber's
sweaty palm pressing him to stillness to avoid drawing blood.

jojo was thinking about his tenth birthday. He was study-
ing his ten fingers, thinking of each one as a year. He was think-
ing about jim-boy. It was his birthday last week when he fell
through the air, wagging his hands, trying to fly. He didn't even
scream. Just flapped his arms and fell like a rock. His mom start-
ed bawling so hard she couldn't breathe. They took her to the
hospital in a cop car.

jo jo could taste the hunger that still drove the cat's
tongue into the rat's airy skull. He wanted some of those fries.
jojo was thinking maybe he'd get himself a one-way ticket out
west, do some surfing, and kick back for some eats with mom.

BOB HOLMAN

POEM

Once when I was little I knelt before an onion,
Dug my arms into the ground up to my elbows
And prayed for my fists to turn into potatoes.
The sky was all owls closing in and a sow bug
Waltzed deftly across my eardrum. It went like
This: dunde sklittle mouse. A golden melody
Popped and cascaded, I could not tell inside
Outside. Tongue, tongue lay there a luscious
Cucumber. Gasp. No wonder you were surprised,
As I waited for potatoes, as you paraded
Past like a typewriter. I was certainly surprised.
Then the onion opened and inside was a potato.

JEANETTE REDENIUS

POTATO GARDEN

I remember watching Benjie
from my kitchen window,
my nephew,
four years old,
cupping the potato
in both hands,
lifting it to my mother,
because it was the best.

That day, she put the potato in a pot
of water, and warmed it
all by itself.
When it was ready to eat
my mother eased it open,
mixed in butter and cream cheese.
The steam lifted its salt
through the kitchen,
and Benjie asked, just to make sure
this was the right one.

Inside ourselves,
my family grows gentle as potatoes.

I smell the wet dirt,
raw in my mother's breath.
I see the strong roots in Benjie's eyes.
If you eased us open
you would find
a garden of potatoes
blooming, like the one
my mom and Benjie made
accidentally, delightfully,
from the compost
last summer.

RUDOLFO ANAYA

LA PAPA

In Spanish potato is papa.
As in papas fritas.
Papas in a chile con carne stew.

Papa is not Papá, which is father,
As in he who brings home the papas.

The papas belong to Mamá, who
Carefully peels one and rubs my
Childhood wart with the peel.
Each day I meet her for the
Ritual in the kitchen, and
Day by day the wart disappears.

The frog I picked up and
Carried for days in my pocket
Caused the wart, my papá tells me.
Don't pick up frogs. Now go peel the papas.

Papiar or hechar una papa
Is to snub someone.
As in, "your papá is as ugly

As a papa."

The lowly papa also stings.
This is the way with words.

ROBERT PHILLIPS

"ARSH POTATOES"

"Roscoe's strictly a meat-and-potatoes man,"
was how Grandmother described my late Grandfather.
There never was a dinner, when we went over,
without mashed potatoes—a smooth white mountain

heaped in a blue china bowl. He always had thirds,
topped with gravy, which he called "The Essence."
After grace, he'd point: "Bobby, would you commence
to pass the Arsh potatoes?" His very words.

For years that's what I thought they were called—
not Irish potatoes, but Arsh. It was one
of the few things he got wrong. Farmer's son,
he dropped out in seventh grade to work. Prodigal

energies made successes of his tenant farms,
his timber lands, his downtown stores, real estate.
Early he amassed a fortune in the aggregate,
was accorded great respect. With his charm,

he was reelected Town Council president three
times. He was proud of his resemblance to Harry Truman,

and of his black Buick, traded-in every two
years. Last night we attended a black-tie country

club supper. "Country" club? That manicured fairway
in no way resembles the landscape he tamed in his youth.
So I smile, don't worry about being thought uncouth:
"Would you commence to pass the Arsh potatoes?" I say.

BRIAN DALDORPH

SPUDS

Now if'n yous go on a motor trip
be sure that you'll be takin' a spud with you,
my grandmother would say.
And not a little spud, no, a big'n,
big as a pig's tit.
And it's not an English spud you'll be takin'
but a fine Oirish one!
Cuz when yous get a hole in your fool tank
and it springs a leak like the Royal Navy,
yous c'n plug it with a spud.
And if'n your windscreen gets dairty
and your woyper gets broken, why,
slice the spud in half and clean the screen,
works better than a spoonge!
An' t' get back at some dairty rotter
yous c'n stuff spud up his exhaust poipe!
An' if'n yous get t' starving why,
yous can eat raw spud an' be glad of it,
thinkin' on the Great Famine.
Still it's best that yous have a bunch o' spuds along,
cuz if'n you run out of petroleum

in the middle of nowhere,
yous can distil your potatoes
an' make it home on potheen.

---

potheen, whiskey from illicit still

ANGELA DE HOYOS

LONG LIVE THE POTATO: ¡VIVA LA PAPA!

(because we have
no *spelling* problems)

… To borrow from the song: In Spain,
it's sí sí; in France, it's oui oui; but in
América-AMERICA, it's *yes mucho yes*.
Let's talk taco, as in *Papas* con Huevo,
Papas con Chorizo, *Papas* con Jamón,
yes mucho yes, *Papas* in the White House,
as in Irish Stew for lunch.

… Not to push the point, but
if a handsome blue-eyed politician
(unaware of his imminent demolition)
had, even momentarily,
put aside his one-track mind
concerning the English-Only concept,
it's ten-to-one he would not have committed
the faux pas of the century…

You see, Castilian Spanish
(and blesséd be the mother who rocked
the collective cradle that gave us the living

language: legacy of the Iberians, the Phoenicians,
Carthaginians, Greeks, Celts, and the *Latin*
Romans—Ay, *los Católicos, Apostólicos*
Romanos—the Visigoths, the French,
Germans, Arabs and, Papa always said,
let's not forget our Sephardic Jews,
those workabee Grandee cool-cats always
bizzy bizzy bizzy doing their own thing…

And shhhhhh!…You won't find this
ancient secret in your Bible, much
less in your history book, but legend has it
that the Spanish language was conceived
by migrant Conjunto angels…Uh huh…
born right up there in the cumulus humilis
comfort of heaven…
                         Actually, they
had been singing *a cappella* all along, but one
day they were called to perform on a *high*
cloud, and—¡'sus!—they stumbled
on a Spin-Me-Ready electric bass, a lost & found
user-friendly drum, a smiling button-type
accordion, a culturally-sensitive bajo sexto,
and—¡ay *caramba!*—the angel-music language
was born…
                         But forget the facts; and the myths)—
Spanish is a language written *naturally*

(como Dios manda), phonetically produced
pronounced and *alabado*. No mistakes; period.

Ergo, in Spanish (if you know the Queen's
Spanish), the potato poses no problem.

In Spanish, the potato shall always be
simply what it is: LA PAPA.

RICHARD KOSTELANETZ
DESIGNED BY IGOR SATANOVSKY

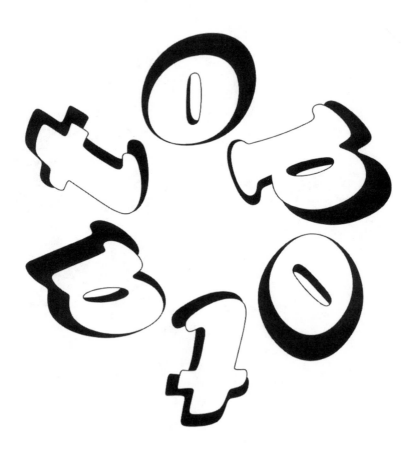

JIM BARNES

THE AMERICAN HERITAGE POTATO

Lying just under *potation*,
to which it is most assuredly related,
claim the Muscovites,
and somewhat above *Potawatomi*,
to whom its spiritual qualities are well known,
this edible tuber is even often supposed to be in *pot-au-feu*,
though the French disclaim it.

In the raw it is
as passive as a dropped fat plum.
It is there for the taking,
incapable of rolling away
because of the nature of its eyes.
No two are alike, unlike the plum,
which is ranked pages above it
and is much sweeter. But you know this,
after having looked up the plural of both:
that both contain an e if you go way back.

Vodka has that potatory taste.
So too does Choctaw chock.
I'm talking *pomme de terre* here
(and its fermentation and distillation)

which has made so many of us sing
and just as many dance.

You can call it *potahto* in America if you want,
but not in the company of a Potawatomi
or a Choctaw who has tasted its higher essence.

JAMES BERTOLINO

AMERICAN POETRY

A poetry sudden as rain flood
down dry-wash creeks

that arrives
fist-rich
where philosophy meets dirt

where gravity pulls green strings
from sunlight

that knows the wisdom of potato,
the water-solid erection
of the princely celery,
the cash-crop eloquence of wheat

a poetry that hoards silence
like a mushroom,
quaking,
invincible white.

Lorca Peress.
A Basket of Potatoes after Cezanne, 1997.
Computer drawing, Microsoft Word 6.0.

Seeing a Basket of Lobelia the Color of a Bathrobe

in the galley of a barge

At that time I read a book about a girl prone
to perfection: her mother had just died.
As she prepared her first supper, she tried
to peel each potato so that not one eye
remained—a perfection of paring. And I,
who also often prepared supper for
my father in my mother's absence, power-
fully attached myself to that girl's unsparing
idea of the world, brooking no mistakes, daring
those still alive to rise to her new standard.
Even I couldn't come up to it, lured
though I was by the thought that my goodness
would prevent all evil, even the drunken mess
our family was in: I was about to cry out,
rupturing our world. Tranquilized, I whirled
in a bath of remorse, then curled

in mother's bathrobe, blinking my potato eye
through the haze of a drug she gave me
—my father's Librium—at a loss for what
else to do, since I wept uncontrollably,

begging her to leave my father and save
all our lives, though there we all stayed.
Now baskets of perfect lobelia fly by,
each flower bathrobe blue, with one white eye.
I peel potatoes below, looking out the little
galley window at their blue, untranquilized,
having left that house so long ago. *Now Dear Miss,
you wanted perfection* ... and found it, whittled
down to a book you couldn't obey. *Be good,*
but leave each potato her imperfect eye,
because something must be left to cry
the tears stored in roots brought out for food.

LAURE-ANNE BOSSELAAR

THE CELLAR

I want my father to stop sending me down there
to fetch his daily gin, and potatoes for supper.
But there's no saying no to him, and no more places to hide:
he's found them all. Outside, the cellar's rusted door
stains my hands as I yank it open, scraping a branch
that whips back, grabbing at me—like he does.

Six stairs stop by a second door, with a hasp
and a slit between two thick planks. I press my face to it,
whisper to the bottles and potatoes: *Go away, I'm coming!*
But how can they? We're all dammed in this big
brick house in Antwerp, and I'm the *Kapo*,
I have no choice: it's them or me.

I kneel in the cellar, pray: *Don't let me separate
families, don't let me kill a child . . .* then inch
toward the shelves—and reach. Sometimes
I think I hear a moan, a sob; sometimes it's a child's wail
so exactly like mine I think it comes out of me—so I quickly
put the thing back: *I'm sorry, I'm sorry.*

The worst are the potatoes. I know exactly

how they lived before, rooted deep in wild, salted polders,
where lapwings titter between cattails and winds,
where rows of loam run past the horizon—
and here they are now, uprooted and cluttered in crates,
limbs groping for a wedge of light from a cellar door.

But then, from up there, comes father's call, weary, irked,
with that pitch and threat in the last vowel of my name.
I grab the gin, the potatoes, hold them as far as I can from my body,
run up, throw them on the table, and escape to my room
where I stand pounding my ears with my fists so as not to hear
yet another cry for mercy.

DIANE WAKOSKI

THE DUCHESS POTATOES

my people grew potatoes,
my hair is lanky and split edged and dishwater
blonde.
My teeth are strong but yellowish
I have little eyes
I am fleshy without muscles
my energy is thin and sharp like gravy
but I crawl into bed as if I were pulling a counter of rubies
over me,
dream past all my lower class barbed wire
walk down the street in a silk glove
try to scrub myself to an aristocratic bone,
and always come back to the faded colors,
lumpy shape;
you wonder why I refuse to type well like my mother,
or iron and mend clothes like my grandmother,
am offended by your boorish father
whose only virtue is that he's tended a machine faithfully
for 35 years and
supported
your beautiful mother
her strange children

he is a ghost of the peasant in me
of ugly linoleum floors
and a starchy diet. And I,
peasant,
have no compassion for the lumps,
the lumpy mashed potatoes
that weren't beaten with enough butter and milk.
and made so fine
so fine
they were called "Duchess"

MEG HUBER

Potato Cellar

Stretched out on a roof
set into a hillside,
drying between dips,
wet suits against shingles,
black sand-speckled shingles
to give sure footing,
roof-heat releasing itself
into our bathing suits.

On this roof, as yesterday,
the two of us alone.
Below us, behind the door
all those baskets of potatoes,
leftovers of a crop never used,
kept just in case,
then left to age.

I saw your hand adjust tan trunks,
the way you did a day ago.
This time I must not open
the strap of my suit
for better tanning,

must not ask you again
"What is down there?"

But my body cannot unlearn.
I try to dig my toes
into black shingles
and hope I do not fall.
This time we must not
open the door,
nor spread clean quilts
to soften the floor
beneath our backs.

LELAND BARDWELL

LILA'S POTATOES

They asked me to write a poem
about Lila's potatoes
I thought about the eighteen forties
I thought about watercress
I thought about weeds
but they were black
my plants were black
lazy beds, they said, were OK.

I had spent my life in lazy beds
one way and another—lazy beds
in and out of lazy beds.

They'd got me everywhere
when I slept in different towns,
places, seas, —another child
lazy beds, they said, were OK in the famine.

I saw my plants—black—leaves black
stalks black—lazy beds, they said—
in the famine—lazy beds.

So I made kids in lazy beds—strapping women
all from lazy beds—eight altogether
they got jobs in underground London pubs,
strip halls—make-believe—run around
and ended up in lazy beds all eight of them.

Lazy beds make black potatoes—Lila's potatoes
have the blight—lazy beds—Lila's potatoes
they got the blight.

Then Seamus took the bad luck out of it.
It was the sun, he said, caused it.
I often wondered what caused all my children.
I'm glad it was the sun.

WYATT TOWNLEY

SWIMMING LESSON

Go under.
Put your whole head in
like the potato that grows
below the feet, below
concrete and the cars
that carry us.

We get up and dress up
and build up and grow
up. The potato grows down.
It underlies everything
we have made
or said, or haven't.

The potato shows us
where we are
heading. Dive in. Put
your whole life
into it.

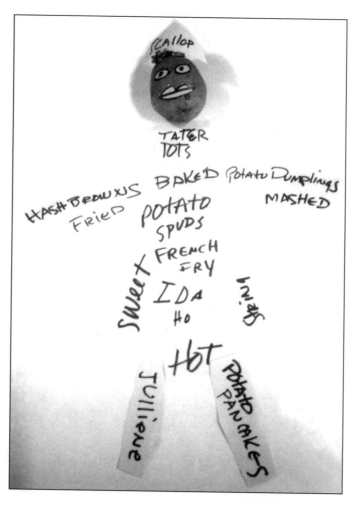

Philomene Bennett.
Hot Potato, 1997.
Mixed Media.

ANN SLEGMAN

Sex and the Single Spud

Hot. Steaming hot.
Straight from the oven, hot.
Skin giving way to skillet,
split wide open,
burn your fingers, hot.
A pad of yellow puddling
into a fluffy, white middle.
A dollop on top, vistas of texture,
mounds and dips of smoothness.
Could I ever leave my lovely young one,
the root of all tenderness,
mashed, hashed, sliced, and cottage
fried? All I can say is this—
it can't get much better
than when I am romancing
the spud.

VIRGINIA R. TERRIS

ROOTS: TO MY DAUGHTER

You told me you were growing potatoes
in your small backyard in a small city
on another coast and I wondered why
seeing you could just go to the corner grocery
and buy a five-pound bag. But then
buried like the tubers themselves
came back as in a dream the way
Father dug up the stony ground
on the slope behind our house
in a wilderness where deer browsed
and Mother cut the eyes of one potato
after another and together the two of them
bent above the earth. Ancient figures.
Their hands covering the eyes with earth.
Waiting for the first bud. The first frost.
For you who never knew them in your faraway place
the ritual goes on. The roots,
burgeoning in the dark,
as if planting themselves.

DONNA TRUSSELL

CHOICE

Potatoes were a delicacy
in my mother's
house, along with canned
corn and, in a rare
gourmet moment, LeSeur
young peas in their tiny
can with silver wrapper. Ah,
that's what *those* people eat,
I thought. My first
date dazzled me with choice
of sour cream, chives
and bacon on my baked
potato. My my! This
is how *those* people
live. He went back to them
of course and there were no
more dates. Just my mother
and her back-burner
skillet of grease, my sister
laying plans for a future
in food stamps, my brother,
his box of Cap'n Crunch

never far away, and me
and my secret stack
of silver wrappers
and my Weigh-Mor
wafers (chalk? ground bone?)
and the occasional
potato.

PATRICIA CLEARY MILLER

Molly O'Rourke Cleary Explains

We were aristocrats in Clare,
Tipperary, Killarney, Kildare.
We garnished our baked potatoes
with bitter Spanish marmalade.
In French boarding schools we studied
literature and embroidery.
I'm sure we had castles and gardens
and forests, and we rode to the hounds.

I'm sure that Patrick, my papa,
came over here for adventure,
and Catherine, my mama, got bored
in Killarney and ran off with
her nanny, whose beau had sailed away
for Saint Louis, where Patrick, with
his bright sapphire eyes and black moustache,
though as old as her father, steamed

Catherine up the wide Missouri
to the Town of the Kanz, the land
of "The People of the South Wind."
They watched the first bridge, for the first

railroad, and started Delmonico's
Hotel, and built the huge stone house
on new Linwood Boulevard, and then

Mama and I dressed like sisters
in white lace gowns and wide feathered
hats, and cook made *pommes frites* and new
American scalloped potatoes
and we all spoke French. But they never
told Irish stories, though we were
always aristocrats, I'm sure.

DENNIS FINNELL

BELLADONNA

Apparently, my people begin and end in Iowa,
with one Mary Keenan who suddenly
showed up in Council Bluffs, ready to scrub
the prairie from their duds and oak floors.

Beyond her, the tribe exists in a fog bank,
the clouds of paradise to some,
gruel to others. They are all anonymous,
except in a general Irish way, faceless

without the luxury of portraits handed down.
They mill around, waiting to shuffle this way
as Mary has, fog parting like parlor drapes,
her carpetbag shifted from hand to hand.

Packed inside are some heartbreaking things,
I just know, from the old country.
Name them, a general nostalgia commands.
They're heavy enough, heavy enough.

What I focus on, want to heft in my
real hands, are the potatoes hidden

in her bag, bound in rags like small mummies,
the eyes beginning to sprout. For her

they mean food, hope, or a last mercy stroke:
seed potatoes for the Iowa spring,
raw ones in winter if no floors need scrubbing,
or the lethal eyes if winter fails.

Never eat the eyes, my mother told me
as she peeled spuds, skins coiling
off like party streamers. I never have,
nor downed bleach with its skull and crossbones,

played chicken, my neck on the track,
or roulette with a real pistol.
I can't say if eating the eyes of potatoes
can kill, or how our family warning began.

Maybe with Mary's last winter, the last
parlor floor in Council Bluffs cleaned,
spring just a memory of chlorophyll,
and the plain potatoes, their eyes, mercy.

There is no work here, Mary.
Go back into whatever the fog is, to faces
more real to you than any descendant's here.
However stunning your face,

the flowers of potatoes, *Solanum tuberosum*,
might kill. It's wrong conjuring you,
beautiful lady. Give us peace,
a homely thing, mostly water and edible.

JASON SANTALUCIA

SUSTENANCE

> *Then his wife said to him,*
> *Do you still persist in your integrity?*
> Job 2:9

It should have been enough that we were poor
and had to fight over money all the time.
Should have been enough that I was too distracted
to pay attention those mornings you woke
to the poverty of our life alone
in that valley of frozen stones with prayers
whispered over every meal of milk and potatoes.
It was a kind of purity, I said, and believed it.

TRISH REEVES

OF POTATOES

We didn't plan our lives this way—
to be taken by the plate
of potatoes, glass of beer,
the bed that came after
always asking for us
to give to love
as if it were a charity
that would cost us no more
once we threw ourselves like a coin
into the great world of need
and declared ourselves
more blessed.

We, the bitten and bounced back
casting the same gold coin, still
wanting the blessing,
still wanting to have a bit more
than the poor.

DAVID CITINO

FAMINE

All over Ireland, survivors held wakes
to keen away the departing, swoll-bellied specters

boarding black ships bound for hell or America.
You can't blame the potato, root-fruit

swaddled in rags, grimacing mug of tough kid
shoved hard in dirt. Landowners, whose law

forbade even the gathering of the manor's twigs
for a fire, flung it at the peasants, swill

for the troughs. When it rotted under fields
into plague's stink, the poor understood,

as they sometimes do, they'd asked too little,
waited a potato too long, prayed a day too hard.

JUDY LONGLEY

FAMINE'S END

Reassured when the moon's pale flesh
curves over trees anchoring our field,
we kneel at trenches, hands silvered
by light, bury tubers as if to fill
our lost children's hungry mouths.

Before bed, warmed by the oily glare
of our lamp, a few potatoes
miraculously steaming in a wooden bowl,
our bodies slump against the table.
Not many left to share this weariness,
the faint taste of earth in each bite.

Holy Mother of Potatoes, your slow
rotation of black and gold reflects
our own estate. Bless our crop
planted in your beneficent glow,
bless those who sleep in faith
of your return. And when we lie down
in the place of potatoes, heads burrowing
into the dark, let us nurture new vine.

MARGARET BLANCHARD

BEFORE THE HUNGER: MEGAN'S BLESSING
as she prepares a meal for the other nuns

What an awful dream,
potatoes becoming stones
as we pulled them out of the earth,
hardening in our hands like mud,
turning white,
round, smooth like bones.
And when we put them in the fire
to cook, they cracked.

Thank God the potatoes
in this sack are still alive.
Aren't you a beauty?
Earth still clings to you,
precious root,
who grew inside her womb.
After you were pulled from her,
she let you go reluctantly.

Let me hold you up for blessing
as the priest does the sacred bread.
Please don't turn to stone,

faithful old soul,
our staff, our life, God's special
gift to us, brown
and simple as we've become
since they stripped us of our trees,
hidden underground as we've been
since they stole the surface from us
and taxed us for standing on it.
Like our heart which beats on unseen
you nourish us, feeding all.
Your blind eyes have seen
greener days and richer soil,
like ours which now see more
than they dare tell.

They call you plain, even
ugly, but we know the grace
which comes through you,
as fully as in their fancy
foods, as cleanly as through
our own sweat, not someone
else's blood.

God's spirit unites you
even as I chop you apart,
so after we plant your pieces
you can become whole again—
not once or twice but many times,

loaves and fishes multiplied.
Into the pot now go
to mingle with the other
wonders of creation,
carrot, onion, cabbage.
Oh Lord, we need look no further
than a stew to witness
your glory.

MARY KAY RUMMEL

LETTER TO A FORMER MOTHER SUPERIOR

In a drawer in the kitchen
potatoes kneel like fisted nuns
foreheads on the damp floor
like the woman who puts time in a bank
then grows so aware of seconds passing
she feels the earth begin to spin
she lies on a couch and counts flies
in a dark corridor she's a half opened hand

Dear mother and sisters
I must confess
last week I broke silence
fifteen hundred times
and I still break it
slice it like a potato
until the white root of silence
stares at me from the floor

In a dream I give a poetry reading
look up to find the eyes of my friends
but the audience is all nuns
white faces folded in stiff wings

eyes   beards
they come to claim me
these tellers of silence

ANNA MORTÁL

The Cork Examiner, December 4, 1846: More Starvation

> "…They were in a state of hunger bordering on starvation,
> but how the bodies came into the dyke of water, whether
> by accident or design on the part of the mother, we have
> no evidence to show. "
>
> —The Jury's Verdict

'Twas the sight of my Bridey's hand, chewed
to the bone when we'd fallen asleep by the barn-side.
We'd eaten the last good potato two days ago, given us
by the house of Hugh Muldowney at Corbetstown.
The rats was as hungry as us. It was them as much
as hunger, if not more so, made me mind up:
the pain hadn't waked her. And the little one
barely rousing now, stone gray with cold.
So I led us down the bank to the dyke,
and I bade the girl sit while I took the babe in
till the waters came to my breasts, and I rocked him
at my waist, like, gentle, with a bit of lullaby,
then let him float on. Bridey came on her own.
Rock me too, Ma, she said, and she slided in
and we held to each other, then sat down together
in the wet and you know, it was warmer there.
We took in the water like soup, our old rags

blossoming wide around us like blue robes of Mary,
our breath the mingling silver of bells, ringing just
sweet as anything I'd ever heard.

DAVID DONNELL

POTATOES

This poem is about the strength and sadness of potatoes.
Unknown in Portugal or China, England or France,
untasted by the legions of Hannibal or Caesar,
hardy, simple, variable tuber; plain dusty brown,
North Carolina, New Brunswick, Idaho,
of the new world, passed over by the Indians
who preferred the bright yellow of corn, its sweetness,
the liquor they made from it, pemmican and wild cons mush.
The potato was seized upon by the more spiritual Puritans
while their companions were enraptured
by the beauty of New World tobacco, cotton and squash.

The Puritans recognized something of themselves in the pale
potato. Its simple shape reminded them of the human soul;
the many eyes of the potato amazed them. They split it
in half and saw the indivisibility of man;
they looked at the many eyes of the potato
and saw God looking back at them.
Potatoes like many different kinds of soil, resist cold weather,
store well in cool cellars and are more nutritious than beets.
Potato dumplings became the pièce de résistance of eastern Europe.
They developed a considerable number of useful proverbs.

For example: "Love is not a potato, do not throw it out the window."
Or the famous Scottish lament—"What good is he to me?
For three days he has not even brought me a potato."

The potato is modest and develops its indivisible bounty
under the ground, taking from the ground some of its color
and just enough skin to resist an excess of moisture.
It can be harvested easily by young boys and girls working
in rows with bushel baskets and pausing at lunch
to lift up their skirts and make love under the fences.
Truckloads of potatoes can be sent to every part of the world.
The French make *frites* with them. The Russians make vodka.
The Chinese have white and brown rice but all potatoes are the same.
Potato flour is not as sweet as corn but makes an excellent bread.
In the cellars of poor farmers all over America
the potatoes sit quietly on top of each other growing eyes.

KEN SMITH

THE END OF ALL HISTORY

That all came out jumbled in all the different heads, Napoleon
v. Attila the Hun, Marie Antoinette in bed with Nostradamus,
the Romans agreeing at last to sign the human rights charter at
Runnymede and grant majority rule within two years. And so
forth. Words words words, example: *potato* from Spanish *patata*
from Carib Taino *batata*, meaning unknown; example: *avocado*
from Spanish *aguacate* from Nahuatl *ahuacatl*, meaning testicle.
Oh ar Oi loiks er bit er specerlatin moiself Oi do, the odd ounze
come in roit andy when erz tattyin to do. But yet I think there
must be someone else beside me on this endless field, or am I
all alone, working in the rain, assuring myself my boots don't
leak, asking who makes these gloves, and these shiny metal
buttons stamped ARMY? Someone must weave these blue shirts,
the colour of the sky beyond these clouds, someone must have
invented this language I speak to myself in. Very interesting.
But with all these spuds to pick in the piddling rain I've no more
time to think about it. I've these bags to fill before dark, and
potatoes don't pick themselves.

PERMISSIONS & ACKNOWLEDGMENTS

Biographical Notes

Rudolfo Anaya is the author of *Bless Me Última*. His recent murder mystery novels include *Zia Summer* and *Rio Grande Fall*. He also writes children's books.

Leland Bardwell was born in India. She grew up in Ireland, and traveled widely, living in London and Paris during the 1940s and 1950s; she now lives in Co. Sligo. She is the author of *Dostoevsky's Grave: New & Selected Poems* (Dedalus, 1991).

Walter Bargen's latest books are *Vertical River* (Timberline Press) and *At the Dead Center of Day* (BkMk Press). He won the 1997 Chester H. Jones Foundation Award.

Jim Barnes is Writer-in-Residence at Truman State University. His 1997 books are *On Native Ground: Memoirs and Impressions* (University of Oklahoma Press) and a collection of poems, *Paris* (University of Illinois Press). He held a Camargo Foundation Fellowship in 1996.

Marvin Bell lives in Iowa City, Iowa, and Port Townsend, Washington. The latest of his fourteen books is *Ardor* (*The Book of the Dead Man, Vol. 2*). Born in Center Moriches, he grew up among the potato fields of eastern Long Island.

Philomene Bennett is an artist whose work is included in major collections throughout the United States. She divides her time between Kansas City and Santa Fe. She is in constant search for the truth—the potato got her one step closer.

Dennis Bernstein, an associate editor with Pacific News Service (PNS), writes regularly on issues of human rights and corporate and state abuse of power. His poetry has been featured in *The New York Quarterly*, *Dark Horse*, and *Pulp Smith*. He is the author of a play, *French Fries*.

 James Bertolino won the *Quarterly Review of Literature* Book Award for *Snail River*, his eighth volume of poems. He has received the Book-of-the-Month Club Poetry Fellowship, an NEA Fellowship, and the Discovery Award. He lives on Guemes Island and teaches at Western Washington University.

 Margaret Blanchard's books include: *The Rest of the Deer: An Intuitive Study of Intuition*; *Duet, A Book of Poems and Paintings*; *Restoring the Orchard: A Guide to Learning Intuition*; and *From the Listening Place: Languages of Intuition*. She teaches in the graduate program of Vermont College-Norwich University.

 Robert Bly's most recent poetry collection is *Morning Poems* (Harper Collins, 1997). He has also recently published a book of cultural criticism, *The Sibling Society* (Addison-Wesley, 1996) and *The Soul Is Here For Its Own Joy: Sacred Poems From Many Cultures* (Ecco Press, 1995).

 Michelle Boisseau's second collection, *Understory*, won the 1996 Samuel French Morse Poetry Prize and was published by Northeastern University Press. Her first book is *No Private Life* (Vanderbilt). A former NEA fellow, she is co-author, with Robert Wallace, of *Writing Poems*, 4th ed. (HarperCollins).

 Eavan Boland is one of Ireland's most prominent and influential poets. Her collection *Outside History* (1990, Norton) marked her American debut. This was followed by *In a Time of Violence* (1994) and her book of autobiographical essays, *Object Lessons* (1995), both published by Norton.

Laure-Anne Bosselaar, a native of Belgium, is the author of *The Hour Between Dog and Wolf* (1997, BOA). She is currently translating American poetry into French and Flemish poetry into English. She lives in Cambridge, Massachusetts.

Michael Dennis Browne's most recent book is *Selected Poems 1965-1995* (Carnegie Mellon University Press). He teaches at the University of Minnesota in Minneapolis.

Maxine Chernoff is the author of six books of poems, two collections of short stories, and two novels, most recently *American Heaven.* She is chair of creative writing at San Francisco State University. With poet Paul Hoover, she edits *New American Writing.*

David Citino is professor of English and creative writing at Ohio State University. He is the author of eight collections of poetry, the latest of which is *Broken Symmetry* (Ohio State University Press).

Peter Cooley's latest book is *The Astonished Hours. Sacred Conversations* was published this year by Carnegie Mellon Press. He teaches at Tulane University in New Orleans.

Brian Daldorph teaches English at the University of Kansas in Lawrence. He is editor of *Coal City Review.* His poetry collection, *The Holocaust and Hiroshima: Poems,* was published by Mid-America Press in December 1997.

Regina deCormier is the author of *Hoofbeats on the Door* (Helicon Nine Editions) and translations of poetry for *The Writings of Christine de Pisan* (Persea Books). She has recent work in *American Poetry Review, Salmagundi, The Nation,* and *Claiming the Spirit Within* (Beacon Press).

 Madeline DeFrees lives and writes in Seattle. Her most recent publications of poetry and prose are in *Paris Review, Crazyhorse,* and the *San Diego Weekly Reader.* She is preparing a *New and Selected Poems.*

 Gertrude Degenhardt was born in New York, and grew up in Berlin. She lives and works on the Irish West Coast and in the Rhine Valley. Among her color etchings is a cycle of 90 images, *Women in Music,* which has been published in book form. Her work has appeared in numerous U.S. magazines.

 Angela de Hoyos has written several books of poetry, including *Woman, Woman* (Arte Público Press). Her numerous honors include the San Antonio Poetry Festival 1994/New Words, Poetry Life Achievement Award. She is co-publisher and editor of M&A Editions.

 David Donnell was born in Ontario. His book of new and selected poems, *Settlements* (McClelland & Stewart), won the Governor General's Award for Poetry in 1983. His collection of poems and stories, *China Blues,* won the City of Toronto Book Award in 1993. He lives in Toronto.

 Joseph Duemer lives in upstate New York. His most recent collection of poetry is *Static* from Owl Creek Press. He is the book review editor for *Poetry International* and poetry editor of the *Wallace Stevens Journal.*

Martín Espada's fifth book of poems, *Imagine the Angels of Bread* (W.W. Norton, 1996), won an American Book Award and was a finalist for the National Book Critics Circle Award. A former tenant lawyer, he is currently a professor of English at the University of Massachusetts-Amherst.

 Dennis Finnell won the 1990 Juniper Prize for *Red Cottage* (UMass Press, 1991), in which his poem "Belladonna" appears. His most recent book is *Belovèd Beast* (University of Georgia Press, 1995). He lives and teaches in western Massachusetts.

 Jan Gilbert, a mixed-media artist, was born and lives in New Orleans, where she teaches at Loyola University. Her most recent exhibition was at L'Embarcadère in Lyons, France. She has received grants from the National Endowment for the Arts and Louisiana Division of the Arts.

 Malcolm Glass has published two volumes of poetry and a textbook on writing poetry. A recent Fulbrighter to Slovenia, he directs the writing program at Austin Peay State University. He is currently writing and producing plays.

 Albert Goldbarth received the National Book Critics Circle Award for *Heaven and Earth*, which was followed by *Adventures in Ancient Egypt*. *Beyond* is forthcoming from David Godine. He lives in Wichita, Kansas (well, *somebody* has to), and orders potato skins and twice-baked potatoes whenever he can.

 Elizabeth Goldring is a poet and media/performance artist. She is author of *Without Warning* (BkMk/Helicon Nine Editions) and *Laser Treatment* (Blue Giant Press). She is Senior Fellow at MIT's Center for Advanced Visual Studies, where she is creating visual poetry for people with limited vision.

Ray Gonzalez is a poet, essayist, and editor born in El Paso, Texas. He has written three books of poetry, the most recent *Memory Fever* (1995, BOA Editions, Ltd.), and a memoir. He has edited seventeen anthologies, including *Touching the Fire: Latino Poetry at the Turn of the Century* (1997, Doubleday).

Shea Gordon is an artist living in Kansas City. She has exhibited throughout the United States, Europe, and South America, most recently at the Benjamin Cardoza Law School gallery in New York City. Her work is in major permanent collections.

Eamon Grennan is the author of two recent volumes of poetry, *So It Goes* (Graywolf, 1995) and *Leopardi: Selected Poems* (Princeton, 1997). He teaches at Vassar College. His spud poem appeared in a volume of poems and essays for Peter Russell—a *Festschrift*, published by the University of Salzburg Press.

Seamus Heaney received the 1996 Nobel Prize in Literature. He is the author of *Selected Poems: 1969-1987*, *The Cure at Troy* (1991), *Seeing Things* (1991), and *The Spirit Level* (1996). His most recent book of criticism is *The Redress of Poetry* (1995). He teaches at Harvard University.

H. L. Hix has a new collection of poems, *Perfect Hell*; a collection of essays, *Spirits Hovering Over the Ashes: Legacies of Postmodern Theory*; and a book of criticism, *Understanding W.S. Merwin*.

John Hollander is a poet, critic and Sterling Professor of English at Yale. His most recent book is *The Work of Poetry* (Columbia University Press); his *Selected Poetry* (Knopf) was published in 1993.

Bob Holman has a new collection of poems, *The Collect Call of the Wild* (Holt). He is the editor of two anthologies, *The United States of Poetry* (Abrams) and *Aloud! Voices from the Nuyorican Poets Café* (Holt). He is a partner at Mouth Almighty/ Mercury Records, the poetry label.

 Meg Huber was raised in Ann Arbor, Michigan, in an academic family of writers and musicians. She graduated from Indiana University, where she learned to admire fine writing in all forms.

 Colette Inez teaches at Columbia University. She has won Ford Foundation, Guggenheim, and two NEA fellowships for her work and is the author of eight collections of poetry. Her latest book, *Clemency*, has just been published by Carnegie Mellon University Press.

 Leatha Kendrick has poems in *Kalliope, Connecticut Review, Cincinnati Poetry Review*, among others. She is co-editor of *Wind* magazine and has taught poetry workshops for the University of Kentucky, Morehead State University, and Kentucky Arts Council.

 X.J. Kennedy is the author of several collections of verse, including *Nude Descending a Staircase* and *Dark Horses*, fifteen children's books, and several textbooks, among them *An Introduction to Poetry*, 9th ed. (with Dana Gioia).

 Jane Kenyon was born in Ann Arbor, Michigan, in 1947. She published five books of poetry, including *Otherwise* (1995, Graywolf Press). She also translated the poetry of Anna Akhmatova. She died of leukemia in April 1995.

John Knoepfle is author of nearly twenty volumes of poetry and stories, including *Poems of the Sangamon* (University of Illinois, 1985, reprint 1995). He taught for many years at Washington University, St. Louis University, and Sangamon State University in Springfield, Illinois.

Richard Kostelanetz has published many books of poetry, fiction, experimental writing, and criticism, including *Wordworks: Poems Selected and New* (1993, BOA), *The Old Poetries and the New* (University of Michigan), and *An ABC of Contemporary Reading* (San Diego University Press, 1995).

Denise Levertov is the author of more than twenty volumes of poetry, including *Sands of the Well* (New Directions, 1996), and four books of prose, most recently *Tesserae* (1995). She is also translator of three volumes of poetry. "Fireside Circles" was written for this anthology. She died on December 20, 1997.

Judy Longley was the 1993 Marianne Moore Poetry Prize winner awarded by Helicon Nine Editions, and her first full-length book, *My Journey Toward You*, was published as a result. Recent work has appeared in *Paris Review*, *Poetry*, and *Western Humanities Review*.

Denise Low teaches at Haskell Indian Nations University. She has books of essays and poetry from BkMk Press, Penthe, Cottonwood, Howling Dog, and Mulberry. She received the 1991-93 Kansas Arts Council Fellowship in Literature.

Thomas Michael McDade lives in Monroe, Connecticut, with his wife Carol. He works in Meriden as a computer programmer. His work has most recently appeared in the *Rag Mag Mothers* anthology.

William Matthews is the author of *Ruining the New Road* (1970), *Sleek for the Long Flight* (1972), *Sticks & Stones* (1975), *Rising and Falling* (1979), *Flood* (1982), *A Happy Childhood* (1985), *Foreseeable Future* (1987), *Blues if You Want* (1989), and *Selected Poems & Translations* (1992). He died in 1997.

Patricia Cleary Miller won the Daniel S. Brenner Award for her first book, *Starting A Swan Dive* (BkMk). She was a Poetry Fellow at the Bunting Institute, Radcliffe College, where she wrote *Without Ice Axes*. She is Director of the Creative Writing Program at Rockhurst College.

Philip Miller is co-founder and director of Kansas City's River Front Reading Series and is on the board of The Writers Place. He has eight books of poetry, including *Hard Freeze* (BkMk), and *From the Temperate Zone* (Potpourri). He teaches English at Kansas City Kansas Community College.

Pat Mora has written over fourteen books of poetry, essays, and children's stories, including *Agua Santa: Holy Water* (1996, Beacon Press) and *House of Houses*, a memoir (1997, Beacon Press). A native of El Paso, Texas, she received a National Endowment for the Arts Poetry Fellowship.

Anna Mortál has work in *Best of Libido* (Dell). She co-edited *Tenderness Toward Existence* and *Tomatoes Still Warm* for the Jeffers Room, Tor House Foundation, Carmel. She is a contributing editor for *Caesura*, and is a coordinator for Writers Harvest: The National Reading (Share Our Strength).

Marty Nichols received the 1997 Kansas Governor's Arts Award. She has been an active force in the Kansas City arts community, serving as president of the Philharmonic and Starlight Theatre. She has had many one-woman shows and is in private collections throughout Kansas and Missouri.

Garry Noland uses reconfigured images of plants, animals, and nature at large to serve as metaphors for human action and predicament. He has had many one-person exhibitions of his collages. He was an art reviewer for *Forum* magazine and executive director of the Kansas City Artists Coalition.

Joyce Carol Oates is the author of several poetry collections, including most recently *Tenderness* (Ontario Review Press). Her poems have appeared in *Paris Review*, *Slate*, *The New Yorker*, and *The Yale Review*. She is a member of the American Academy of Arts and Letters.

Nam June Paik was born in Korea and studied music in Germany, where he met John Cage and became engaged in the Fluxus movement of the '60s. He has developed his ideas for the new technology in a new touring exhibition entitled: *The Electronic Super Highway, Nam June Paik in the '90s.*

Elise Paschen received the Nicholas Roerich Poetry Prize for her first book of poems, *Infidelities* (Story Line, 1996). Her poems have been published in *Poetry*, *The New Yorker*, and *The New Republic*, among others.

Molly Peacock, author of four books of poems, including *Original Love* (W.W. Norton & Co.) and *Take Heart* (Random House), and a memoir, *Paradise Piece by Piece* (1998, Riverhead/ Penguin), is co-editor of *Poetry in Motion: 100 Poems from the Subways and Buses*, and a life-long lover of mashed potatoes.

Lorca Peress, a New York-based theatre and visual artist, studied both disciplines at Bennington College. She acts, directs, writes for the stage, and in 1995 received an Inky Award for playwriting from La MaMa, E.T.C. for *Women Under Glass*. She has illustrated a book of dance poems, *Hey Ginger!*

Robert Peters, prolific poet, eminence gris of poetry criticism, actor playwright, dramatist, and memoirist, has published poetry and prose about his origins on a Wisconsin farm. His most recent books include *Hunting the Snark: American Poetry at Century's End* and *For You Lili Marlene: A Memoir of WWII*.

Robert Phillips is Professor of English and former Director of the Creative Writing Program at the University of Houston. He is author of five books of poetry and three of fiction.

Otto Piene, a German-born sky artist, light and environmental artist and painter, is both author and subject of books written and published over the past forty years. He has work in c. 200 museums and public collections worldwide. He is Professor Emeritus of the Center for Advanced Visual Studies at MIT.

Stanley Plumly has a new collection, *The Marriage in the Trees*, which appeared in the spring, 1997, from Ecco Press. He teaches at the University of Maryland.

Dan Quisenberry is the author of two books of poetry: *On Days Like This* and *Down & In* (1998, 1995, Helicon Nine Editions). The former baseball pitcher had poems in *Aethlon, Fan, New Letters, Spitball, Thorny Locust*, and in the anthologies *Poets at Large* and *Fathers*. He died on September 30, 1998.

Rush Rankin has had poems, stories, and essays appear in *Paris Review, TriQuarterly, New Letters, Chelsea* and others. His book *The Postmodern Comedy* was published by Aldus Press, 1993. He teaches writing and theory at the Kansas City Art Institute.

Rochelle Ratner has written thirteen volumes of poems, including *Practicing To Be A Woman: New and Selected Poems* (Scarecrow Press, 1982) and *Someday Songs* (BkMk Press, 1992). She lives in New York City, where she is Executive Editor of *American Book Review*.

David Ray lives in Tucson and won the New Millennium Award for 1997. His collection of poems about New Zealand, *Wool Highways* (Helicon Nine Editions), won the 1994 William Carlos Williams Poetry Prize. His most recent book is *Kangaroo Paws*.

Jeanette Redenius is a graduate of Penn State University, where she earned her B..A. in history. This is her first publication.

Trish Reeves won the Cleveland State University Poetry Center Prize for her book *Returning the Question*. Other awards for poetry include NEA and Yaddo Fellowships. She teaches at Haskell Indian Nations University in Lawrence, Kansas.

Daisy Rhau recently moved from Pennsylvania to the San Francisco Bay area. She has published poems and essays in *New Letters*, *North American Review*, and *Kenyon Review*.

Mary Kay Rummel is the author of *This Body She's Entered* (New Rivers), a Minnesota Voices Award winner. Her poems have appeared in recent issues of *Nimrod*, *Passages North*, and *California Quarterly*. She lives in Fridley, MN, and teaches at the University of Minnesota in Duluth.

Jason Santalucia has taught writing at Penn State University and now is a student at San Francisco Theological Seminary. He has had a poem published in *New Letters* and has received awards from the Academy of American Poets.

Igor Satanovsky, born in Russia, works as a designer and translator in New York City, in addition to co-editing the new literary magazine *Koja*.

Ann Slegman has had poetry, fiction, and articles published in *New Letters, Helicon Nine, Redbook,* and *McCall's*. Her novel, *Return to Sender*, was published by Helicon Nine Editions in 1995 .

Ken Smith lives in Wales and is the author of *A Book of Chinese Whispers* (1987, Bloodaxe Books).

S.B. Sowbel, a long-time resident of Baltimore, now paints and writes in the "snow pocket" of Vermont.

Robert Stewart is the author of *Letter from the Living* (Big Blue Prairie Editions), poems and an essay, with art by Joan Backes; and *Plumbers* (BkMk Press), a collection of poems. He is managing editor of *New Letters* magazine at the University of Missouri-Kansas City, where he also teaches.

Kristen Struebing-Beazley eats potatoes in Boston and photographs them on windowsills, couches, mantlepieces, and in other locations. (Cover photograph.)

Arthur Sze recently received a John Simon Guggenheim Memorial Foundation Fellowship. A new book, *The Red-shifting Web: Poems 1970-1997*, was published in 1998 by Copper Canyon Press.

Virginia R. Terris has published three collections of poetry as well as criticism and reviews. Her most recent volume is *Meaningful Differences: The Poetry and Prose of David Ignatow* (University of Alabama, 1994).

Roderick Townley fled the New York magazine world for a supposedly simpler life in Kansas. His publications include a novel, several nonfiction books, two volumes of poetry, and a critical work. He is the editor of a forthcoming essay anthology, *Night Errands: How Poets Use Dreams* (University of Pittsburgh Press).

Wyatt Townley, since she was a little girl, has eaten mashed potatoes on her birthday. Her poems and essays have appeared variously in magazines ranging from *Paris Review* to *Newsweek*. Her first book of poems, *Perfectly Normal*, was a finalist for the Yale Series of Younger Poets.

Donna Trussell has published poems and stories in *Poetry, Chicago Review, TriQuarterly, North American Review*, and other magazines. She is a native Texan who now lives in Kansas City. Her short story "Fishbone" has appeared in several anthologies, most recently in *Texas Bound* (1998, SMU Press).

Lequita Vance-Watkins is a California Artists Fellowship for Literature recipient, PEN Center West finalist and the co-editor/ translator of *White Flash/Black Rain: Women of Japan Relive the Bomb*. She is Director of Caesura Center for Literary Arts and editor of *caesura literary journal*.

 Gloria Vando received the 1998 Poetry Society of America's Alice Fay Di Castagnola Award for her manuscript *Shadows & Supposes*. She is the author of *Promesas: Geography of the Impossible* (Arte Público Press) and *Caprichos* (Howling Dog Press). She is publisher and editor of Helicon Nine Editions.

 Peter Viereck won a Pulitzer Prize for *Terror and Decorum* (Greenwood Press) and is the only American scholar to receive Guggenheim Fellowships in both poetry and history. In each genre he has written eight books. His spud poem is from his book *Tide and Continuities* (University of Arkansas Press, 1995).

 Dina von Zweck is the author of thirty-one books (fiction and non-fiction) and the recipient of numerous grants and awards. She has written screenplays and teaches screenwriting workshops in New York City. She can be reached by email: dina@escape.com.

 Diane Wakoski's most recent work is *Argonaut Rose* (Black Sparrow Press, 1998). She has written over twenty books of poetry, including *Emerald Ice: Selected Poems 1962-1987*.

 Mary S. Watkins, photographer, is currently exhibiting her "Stereographs" and developing a market for her "Hearts for All Seasons," a collection of natural heart-shaped objects. Her photographs recently appeared in *New Letters*, *The New York Times*, and in a photo essay in *Kansas City Magazine*.

Opal Whitely grew up in nineteen lumber camps in Oregon. She began her diary when she was six years old, reconstructed it in 1920, and died in England in 1991. **Jane Boulton** lives in Palo Alto, California. In addition to adapting *Opal: The Journal of an Understanding Heart*, she has written a novel.

Susan Whitmore is the executive director of The Writers Place in Kansas City and teaches English at the University of Missouri-Kansas City. She is the author of *Invisible Woman* (Singular Speech Press) and *The Sacrifices* (Mellen Poetry Press).

Richard Wilbur has won two Pulitzer Prizes for his poetry, and in 1987-88 served as the second Poet Laureate of the United States. His translations of Molière and Racine have been widely produced in English-speaking countries.

David Williams is the author of *Traveling Mercies*, a poetry collection. His work is discussed in *Memory and Cultural Politics: New Approaches to American Ethnic Literatures*, edited by Amritjit Singh, et al.

Robley Wilson has in his lifetime moved from Maine to Iowa to Florida, where he now lives. His chapbook, *A Walk Through the Human Heart*, was published by Helicon Nine Editions.

Thomas Zvi Wilson is a poet and artist who emigrated from New York to the Midwest in 1974. BkMk Press recently published his collection of poems, *Deliberate and Accidental Acts*.

INDEX

OTHER OUTSTANDING BOOKS BY HELICON NINE EDITIONS

WILLA CATHER FICTION PRIZE WINNERS
One Girl by Sheila Kohler, selected by William Gass
Climbing the God Tree, a novel in stories by Jaimee Wriston Colbert, Dawn Raffel, judge
Eternal City, stories by Molly Shapiro, selected by Hilary Masters
Knucklebones, stories by Annabel Thomas, selected by Daniel Stern
Galaxy Girls: Wonder Women, stories by Anne Whitney Pierce (second printing),
selected by Carolyn Doty
The Value of Kindness, stories by Ellyn Bache (second printing), selected by James Byron Hall
Sweet Angel Band, stories by R.M. Kinder, selected by Robley Wilson

MARIANNE MOORE POETRY PRIZE WINNERS
Flesh by Susan Gubernat, selected by Robert Phillips
Diasporadic by Patty Seyburn, with an introduction by Molly Peacock, judge
Prayers to the Other Life by Christopher Seid, selected by David Ray
A Strange Heart by Jane O. Wayne (second printing), selected by James Tate
Night Drawings by Marjorie Stelmach, selected by David Ignatow
My Journey Toward You by Judy Longley, selected by Richard Howard
Women in Cars by Martha McFerren, with an introduction by Colette Inez, judge
Black Method by Biff Russ, with an introduction by Mona Van Duyn, judge

FICTION
Return to Sender, a novel by Ann Slegman
Italian Smoking Piece: with Simultaneous Translation by Christy Sheffield-Sanford

POETRY
On Days Like This by Dan Quisenberry
Wool Highways by David Ray, winner of the 1994 William Carlos Williams Award
Without Warning by Elizabeth Goldring
Hoofbeats on the Door by Regina deCormier, with an introduction by Richard Howard

ANTHOLOGIES
Poets at Large: 25 Poets in 25 Homes, ed. by H.L. Hix
Helicon Nine Reader: A Celebration of Women in the Arts, ed. by Gloria Vando Hickok